Kerry Morris

THE UNCHRISTIAN CHRIST

Modern Christianity & Jesus of Nazareth

Copyright © 2023 W. Kerry Morris
All Rights Reserved
Paperback ISBN 978-1-7335491-1-0

Holy Bible references are taken from the translations below:

Holy Bible: Common English Bible. 2011. Nashville, TN: Common English Bible. (CEB)

Holy Bible: New Living Translation. 2015. Carol Stream, IL: Tyndale House Publishers. (NLT)

Holy Bible: Complete Jewish Bible. 2018. New York, NY: WW Norton. (CJB)

The Holy Bible: The Amplified Bible. 1987. 2015. La Habra, CA: The Lockman Foundation.

Cover Design by Beth Burrell

Table of Contents

Dedication	vii
Acknowledgments	ix
Christ or Christians?	1
Sources and Humble Assumptions	9
"Christians Have Too Many Rules" The Seven-Word Law	13
"Christians Don't Accept the Outcasts" The Case Of The Samaritan Woman	19
"Christians Are Not Very Diverse" Choosing the Different	25
"Christians Are So Angry" *Part 1:* When Jesus Chose Anger	31
"Christians Are So Angry" *Part 2:* When Jesus Said No to Anger	39

"Christians Just Want Political Power"
    A Different Kind of Kingdom   45

"Christians Don't Like Gay People"
    Knowing and Loving   55

"Christians Want To Take Away Reproductive Rights"
    The Humility of Not Knowing Everything   65

"Christians Are So Judgmental"
    Part 1: Holding the Scales   75

"Christians Are So Judgmental"
    Part 2: Wielding the Sword   81

"Christians Want To Enforce Their Views on Everyone Else"
    Leading Like a Shepherd   87

"Christians Expect Me To Believe Everything in The Bible"
    God or Book About God?   93

"Christians Do Not Believe in Science"
    The Faith of an Open Mind   113

"Christians Feel Like They Are Under Attack"
    So What?   125

"Christians Think There Are Three Gods but Really One God?"
    The Trinity Relationship   135

"Christians Think Jewish People Need To Be Converted"
    The God Jesus Prayed To   141

"Christians Are Hypocrites"
    Part 1: Relationship With Other People   151

"Christians Are Hypocrites"
    Part 2: Relationship With God   157

Mini-Christs and Major Truth   167

Endnotes   175

Dedication

To every heart who deeply longs to connect with the divine.
To every soul who inadvertently blocks the view of heaven.
To the God who loves them both immeasurably.

Acknowledgments

Special thanks to my amazing friends and family who were so generous with their time, feedback and prayers as this project came together - Katie Morris, Marie Dias, Mark Pifer, Dr. Leigh Hamby, John Warnock, John McGriff, and Hubert Kang.

I am also deeply grateful to every friend, acquaintance, pastor, author, artist, and thinker who has shared their thoughts and questions on the divine. This is especially true for those with whom I disagree.

As iron sharpens iron, so a friend sharpens a friend.
Proverbs 27:17 (NLT)

1

Christ or Christians?

From 2014 to 2021, the percentage of adults in the U.S. who identified themselves as Christian declined from 78% to 63%. This means about 49 million fewer people associated themselves with the religion built on the teachings of Christ.² This decline has been seen to varying degrees across all Christian denominations, Catholic and Protestant, mainline and evangelical.

Christianity has a problem.

But during the same time period, the percentage of people identifying as part of other religions barely moved, only increasing from 5% to 6%. So, it is not as if there is a wave of Christians converting to Islam or Buddhism. Where did all these former Christians go? The data suggests most of them became religious "Nones." The percentage of the population who do not associate with any religion increased from 16% to 29% during this period. So, of the 49 million people who a decade ago would have called themselves Christian, 42 million call themselves nothing at all.

They have left formal religion altogether. This suggests that there is not a vast swath of Christians who have become enamored of another faith or find another religion's view of God suits them better.

Christianity's problem is not other religions.

At the same time, it is difficult to find any broad hatred for the person of Jesus of Nazareth. Christians refer to him as Christ, a title derived from a Hebrew word meaning "anointed by God" or Messiah. While people of other religions and the non-religious question the divinity of Jesus, there seems to be almost universal appreciation for his teachings and how he lived his life. Almost everyone seems to admire his willingness to stand up to the existing power structure of his day, to advocate for those diminished by society, to endure great personal suffering for his beliefs. Ask a search engine, "Why do people dislike Jesus?" and you must scroll for pages before you find any specific complaint. Everyone from Gandhi to Nietzsche has said good things about Jesus.

Christianity's problem is not Jesus Christ.

I am a follower of Jesus, and I try to live life according to his teachings. But I spend most of my life around people who view the Christian faith with indifference, skepticism, or outright hostility. In those contexts, although I openly identify myself as a follower of Jesus, it is often a negative to use the term "Christian." This is because the term "Christian" to many of those who are outside the faith has become a label that means something altogether different from the teachings of Jesus. It increasingly refers to a lifestyle, a political affiliation, advocacy for a specific set of political issues and candidates, or one faction in a culture war. Or put another way, if you ask someone what Christians believe, beyond that Jesus was God, the first few answers are more likely to be a list of political and cultural positions rather than specific things that Jesus taught.

Most of the people I encounter every day are actively trying to be good people, making good choices. However, they generally do not think of Christianity as a means to becoming a good person or making good choices. For many, Christianity is just not relevant or desirable. Yet, I almost never hear any objection to the teachings of Jesus. Rather, the most common reasons for viewing Christianity with indifference or disdain usually are rooted in an impression of Christians, the people associated with this faith, and the religious organizations that represent them.

When you search the internet for "What's wrong with Christianity?" you will find a host of anecdotal comments and detailed research to answer the question.

> "Christians have so many odd rules."
> "Christians do not embrace people who are different."
> "Christians are not very diverse."
> "Christians seem so angry."
> "Christians are so judgmental."
> "Christians are too political."
> "Christians hate gay people."
> "Christians want to take away reproductive rights."

"Christians want to enforce their views on everyone else."
"Christians base everything on some book I don't believe in."
"Christians twist scriptures to manipulate people."
"Christians don't believe in science."
"Christians complain they are under attack."
"Christians think there are three Gods but really one God and that seems odd."
"Christians try to convert Jewish people."
"Christians are just hypocrites."

Of course, all these statements are not true of all Christians. Different Christian sects, Catholic and Protestant alike, have different beliefs and behaviors. Within those organizations, local churches vary in what they teach and the behaviors they expect. And, of course, individual Christians show huge variation in beliefs and behaviors. Because of this, how people perceive individual Christians also varies greatly.

But there are more than enough real examples to demonstrate that the negative opinions listed above are widely held. Misdeeds done in the name of Christianity in our society today, much less throughout history, would fill volumes. When the rest of the world looks at Christians, all too often they do not see people that reflect the teachings and values of Jesus.

Christianity as a religion seems to be caught perpetually in a tug of war. On one side are the Christians who fail to live up to its ideals and who are, therefore, often disliked by society. On the other side is the person of Jesus Christ, who was the perfect adherent to Christian ideals and is almost universally admired by society.

When people think of the religion of Christianity, I suspect their opinion is more likely anchored in their view of Christians who claim to follow that faith, not the Christ whose life inspired it. And if people who call themselves Christians are the lens through which we view Christianity, then it is no surprise that forty million people have turned away from the religion.

It is likely that Christianity's problem is Christians.

At this point we could dive into all the reasons Christians might fall short of the ideals of their faith, or even the standards of morality common to all faiths. Christians are imperfect, fallible humans, after all. But, the purpose of this book is not to defend, explain, or even admonish Christians.

My goal is not to try and redeem the term "Christian" from its negative cultural baggage. Nor is my goal to criticize the Christian community or individual Christians for playing a part in building or reinforcing those negative stereotypes. We are all imperfect. And there are many other voices inside and outside of the faith who are doing the work of calling out those imperfections and recommending a path forward.

Rather than being a book about Christians or Christianity, this is a book about Jesus. My goal in these pages is to better understand the Jesus who Christians claim to follow. I will use modern day impressions of Christians as a lens through which to view

Jesus, a reference point against which to compare. Those who have studied the life of Jesus at length know the end of the story already. All followers of Jesus come up short of his example. But there is still much to learn from the comparison.

Several years ago, I had the pleasure of visiting the world's largest tree, a redwood named General Sherman in California. The first few photos I took of this behemoth did not really convey its size, because there was no sense of scale. But, when I asked my sons, ordinary-sized teenagers, to stand beside it, anyone viewing the photo could gain a new appreciation for the true size of the tree. In this way, I will use modern impressions of Christians as a yardstick in the same frame as the person of Jesus. We will use something we know as a point of comparison to help us learn about something worth understanding more. My hope is that by comparing modern Christians with what we know about Jesus, we can better understand this person who had such a profound impact on humanity.

And understanding who he was is a worthy pursuit. It is impossible to deny the profound impact Jesus had on human history. A poor Jewish carpenter with minimal formal education, and only about three years of public ministry, has inspired the devotion of hundreds of millions of people over the two thousand years since. And the revolutionary ideas he taught about love and justice and equality have impacted the values of the Western world perhaps more than any other single person.

In the pages that follow, I will review the most common complaints society has about Christians and compare them to what we know about the life of Jesus. Are today's Christians really so far removed from the teachings of the one they call God? How different really are today's Christians from the person of Jesus? If we line up all the components that make up the public perception of Christianity, how much is in common with the life and teachings of Christ?

Said another way, would Jesus himself feel at home in the ranks of today's Christians? Or would he be too Un-Christian for the religion that calls him Christ?

2

Sources and Humble Assumptions

Since the goal of this book is to better understand the person of Jesus of Nazareth, it might be an easy reflex to do so through the lens of Christian beliefs. Most Christians believe the Bible to be an infallible source of truth. Christians believe that Jesus was God. And Christians are generally very confident in their interpretation of right and wrong. But if these beliefs are prerequisites for learning about Jesus, then the hundreds of millions of people who are not Christians will likely never learn about him. Attempting to prove the core claims of Christianity is a much different discussion for a much longer book. So, in these pages I will not ask the reader to assume the broader the claims of Christianity are true.

First, I will not ask the reader to assume the Bible is the inspired word of God. Proving that point could fill volumes. And, if our goal is to understand the person of Jesus, we can learn a great deal about him if we just view the Bible as historical literature. This might make some Christians uncomfortable, since so much well-written commentary and theology is heavily seasoned with scripture from all over the Bible. But, almost without exception, non-Christians do not believe the Bible is the word of God. And it seems unreasonable to ask them to believe in a book before they can believe in the God who Christians claim inspired the book. Instead, we will rely on the first-person accounts of the life of Jesus as captured in the books of Matthew, Mark, Luke, and John, as well as other historical accounts of the time. After all, this represents more scripture than the first-century gentile Christ followers around the Mediterranean had at their disposal. The other books of the Bible will be referenced only if they are quoted by Jesus, or they provide insight in the culture in which Jesus lived.

Regardless of which specific books of the Bible we consider, a central theme is God's pursuit of reconciliation with humankind. Christians believe God's desire to connect with people came to a climax with the birth of Jesus of Nazareth, and that Jesus was God come to earth in the form of a man.

Perhaps the most famous passage from the Bible captures the central theme with these words:

> "'God so loved the world that he gave his only Son, so that everyone who believes in him won't perish but will have eternal life. God didn't send his Son into the world to judge the world, but that the world might be saved through him.'"[3]

But for the pages that follow, we will also not assume the divinity of Jesus Christ, that he was God in the form of man. Obviously, this is the foundational belief of the Christian faith. But this book is not about explaining or justifying the Christian faith so much as it is about understanding the person of Jesus. And it is certainly possible to study Jesus without the underlying assumption that he is God. Many, many words have been written to either prove or disprove whether Jesus was divine. And regardless of where one falls on that question, a person's answer is informed by an understanding of how Jesus lived his life and the things that he said. We will focus on expanding that understanding in these pages.

Finally, we will not presume to have all the answers. Often religious discussions are characterized by someone expressing complete confidence in a given conclusion. While there are many things that are certain, there are a great many questions that honest study must admit we just cannot answer conclusively. These unanswered questions do not represent a lack of faith. Rather, they are evidence of faith. A God we can completely understand would not be much of a God at all. And a human who understood everything about all we do not see would not be a human at all. It is okay, even desirable, to sometimes say simply, "I do not know." Being open to the reality of unanswered questions demonstrates humility in the face of an infinite God and an infinite universe, and this open-mindedness reflects a realistic view of the limitations of human understanding.

When this type of difficult question arises in the pages that follow, we will discuss the best evidence available and arguments on both sides of the question. But we will resist the urge to make absolute declarations in the face of missing or seemingly conflicting information. To do any more would be to reduce an infinitely complex divine question into a human-sized simplistic answer. We will aggressively avoid that kind of hubris because it stunts the drive to discover. If we assume we know, we lose the appetite to learn. And anyone who embraces the concept of the divine in any form must surely embrace the humility of this truth: each of us have so much to learn.

3

"Christians Have Too Many Rules"
The Seven-Word Law

"[Christianity] has been used and is still used as a way of forcing obedience from people by threat of God's wrath at non-compliance as well as a way of oppressing and dominating people... [It] has to be viewed as being purposed and created as a way of controlling the masses." [4]

– Post from Quora.com

"There are 1,752 canons, or rules, in Catholic Canon Law." [5]

> *"Clothing should cover all aspects of the chest, mid-section (including sides), and waist to approximately mid-thigh while on campus. Casual dress consists of class dress and/or loose-fitting shorts that come to approximately mid-thigh (sitting or standing)... Rips or tears above mid-thigh must not expose skin. Swimming pool attire should be a modest swimsuit (Men: shorts-style swimsuit, not briefs. Women: one-piece or tankini, no bare midsection)."* [6]
>
> – Liberty University Student Honor Code

> *"15% of Catholics, 16% of Protestants, and 23% of white evangelicals believe consuming alcohol is morally wrong."* [7]
>
> – Pew Research Center

When we hear many Christians talk about their faith, you might get the sense Christianity is just a long list of rules to be followed. Everyone has probably heard of the core Ten Commandments, even though only 14% of Americans can name them all.[8] [9] But if you read the entire portion of the Christian Bible known as the Old Testament, which is essentially the same as the ancient Hebrew Scriptures known as the Torah or Pentateuch, you would find over six hundred different rules to be followed.[10]

Of course, this is nothing compared to the myriad of official and unofficial rules espoused by many Christians today. "You must go to this specific type of church, but not the other one!" "You must vote a particular way." "You must dress a particular way." "You can go to heaven if you ask God to forgive your sins, but you cannot receive communion at our church unless you do this list of other things."

All these rules create several problems. First, they can be overwhelming, even to the most ardent would-be follower of Christ. Even if someone could remember all these rules, who has that kind of will power and diligence? And, let's face it, many of these rules have changed over the years. Jesus literally made wine, but now 15% of his followers claim drinking alcohol is a sin. The original Hebrew law said eating pigs was a sin. But next time you are in a barbecue restaurant, ask how many people there call themselves Christian. This says nothing of the many unofficial rules created by Christians linking faith to specific political policies. There are even some who would argue there is a proper Christian perspective on seemingly secular issues like border security, Social Security reform, and trade policy with China.

All these rules and norms can be overwhelming and frustrating. But the biggest danger of this massively long and frustratingly transient set of rules is that it obscures the much more important simple underlying truths. Beautiful, helpful truths often get lost in a forest of seemingly arbitrary rules. Jesus consistently resisted this rules-based religiosity and was quick to resist those who tried to reduce faith to a list of rules.

On one occasion, Jesus and his friends were walking through a field of grain on the sabbath. The sabbath was one day each week set aside by religious rules as a day of rest, and work of any kind was strictly forbidden. The followers of Jesus were hungry, so as they walked, they picked the heads of grain and ate them.

The religious leaders were quick to criticize what they saw as someone ignoring an important rule that defined their faith.

> "The [religious leaders] said to [Jesus], 'Look, why are they doing what is unlawful on the Sabbath?' But Jesus pushed back, saying 'The Sabbath [rule] was created for humans; humans weren't created for the Sabbath [rule].'"[11]

In other words, religious rules were not put in place by God to control people. They were put in place to help people. God wanted people to rest and not work on the Sabbath, but that did not mean they had to go hungry.

Jesus did not try to leave his mark or demonstrate his power by imposing an extensive list of new rules on people. On the contrary, he cut through centuries of religious bureaucracy and misdirected piety to reduce faith to two simple rules. A religious expert once asked Jesus, "…What is the greatest commandment in the Law?" This was a loaded question since there were hundreds of different rules to choose from. Great debates had been waged among religious leaders around which commands took precedence, and how different commands related to each other. This question was a great way to start a complex and nuanced religious fight.

But Jesus responded, not by complicating, but by simplifying. Jesus replied,

> "'You must love the Lord your God with all your heart, with all your being, and with all your mind. This is the first and greatest commandment. And the second is like it: You must love your neighbor as you love yourself. All the law... depends on these two commands.'"[12]

"Love God. Love your neighbor. Love yourself." The entire law of Jesus can be reduced to seven words. It is beautiful and powerful in its simplicity. Note two things about this seven-word law. First, it is all about relationships. At the core of the teaching of Jesus is a profound sense of connectedness. We are connected to ourselves. We are connected to each other. We are connected to God. The health of those three relationships is paramount. Second, Jesus said each relationship should be based on love. The framework through which we understand the universe should be one of relationship. And the guiding force, the north star of each relationship should be love.

Jesus did not try to regulate and control specific behaviors and actions. He was focused on mindful relationships and loving motives. He taught that if our heart was full of love and we cared about our relationships, then our actions would naturally fall into line. The wisdom and simplicity of this is astounding. Think for a moment of any evil or injustice or pain in the world. Scan the headlines of your local news for a list of horrible things, think about how you have seen one person hurt another or themselves. Then consider whether each could have been prevented by following this seven-word law.

A domestic dispute ends in murder.
A young person commits suicide.
A nation attacks another, killing thousands.
Government officials favor one group to retain power.

In each case, was the perpetrator mindful that they are in relationship with God, a part of something bigger and more divine than a moment of pain or pleasure? Did they love God and embrace that sense of connection?

Was the perpetrator aware of their connection to others, the impact they have on the rest of humanity? And was their motivation driven by a profound sense of love for other people, even those they disagree with?

Did the person have a deep and honest perception of themself? Did they actively seek to get to know themselves better? And, despite the imperfections that plague us all, did they embrace themselves with acceptance and love?

The seven-word law of Jesus is more powerful and comprehensive than any compilation of Christian church rules could ever be. The teachings of Jesus can have an enormously positive impact on the world. But this impact does not come from controlling but by leading. It is born not of compliance with rules but by loving relationships.

4

"Christians Don't Accept the Outcasts"
The Case Of The Samaritan Woman

"I've been threatened (with their hell) called names, invalidated, and lied to by religious people throughout my lifetime. I am one of those 'others' that they treat harshly. Then they have the temerity to turn around and wonder why I hate religion so much."

– Post from Quora.com[13]

"Where Jesus Christ sees a man, though he be an outcast, an outlaw, one condemned by the law of his own country, he sees a human being there – a creature capable of awful sin and terrible misery – but yet, renewed by grace, capable of bringing

wondrous glory... He considers not so much where a man is, but what he is; not what he has learned, or what he is thought of, or what he has done; but what he is. The man is the jewel, the immortal soul is the pearl of great price, which Jesus seeks..."

– *Charles Spurgeon*[14]

Increasingly, there is a public perception that Christians are unaccepting or even outright antagonistic to those of different cultures, different faiths, different morals, even different ethnicities. While many Christians are very tolerant of those who are different, a quick scan of social media will quickly yield a great many examples of those who identify as Christ-followers but are dismissive or antagonistic toward those with a different culture and religion. To make things worse, Christian symbols have been co-opted to support political and cultural movements that isolate, or even outright oppress, those who are different.[15]

In first-century Judea, where Jesus lived, religion was an exclusive club. By all accounts, religious leaders did not socialize with ordinary folk. Priests and rabbis dressed differently, spoke differently. A devout follower of the Jewish faith in those days was expected not to socialize with those from other faiths, to avoid being around those who did not follow the standard rituals for cleanliness, even to avoid interaction with people who had certain ailments. Great care had to be taken not to sully oneself by contact with others who were not fully compliant with religious law.

However, Jesus made a regular practice of embracing the "others." He dined with tax collectors who worked on behalf of the Roman government to extort money from their own people. They were almost universally hated and looked down upon. The first-person accounts of Jesus' life mention him spending a great deal of time with these and all types of sinners, all manner of people who were not compliant with the prevailing religious law.

Perhaps the most compelling example of Jesus reaching out to the "others" is his interaction with a particular Samaritan woman. Jesus had just taken a long journey and sat down by a well to rest. A woman from Samaria came to the well to draw water, and Jesus had an extensive conversation with her. For a Jewish teacher, even this conversation was extraordinary.

This woman was religiously undesirable, from a different faith. Many devout Jews felt Samaritans were a heretical sect since they worshiped in a different place. Also, many Samaritans also worshiped many local pagan gods which was a great offense to the Jewish people, who were staunchly monotheistic.

She was ethnically undesirable. The Samaritans were known to have intermarried with other races in Canaan and were looked down on by devout Jews intent on keeping their race distinct.[16] Good Jews simply did not associate with Samaritans.

She was socially undesirable. This was a woman, at a time in history when women were second class citizens at best, property at worse. A prominent leader could only lower his standing by casually interacting with a woman.

She was morally undesirable. Through the course of their conversation, it became apparent Jesus knew she lived a lifestyle that was highly promiscuous by the standards of the day. She had been married five times and was currently living with a man who was not her husband. A devout person had no business speaking with her, lest he be associated with her sins.

In this one interaction, Jesus broke just about every rule about with whom a devout Jewish person, much less a distinguished religious leader, should interact.

Yet not only did Jesus speak with her, he also took time to get to know her, understand her unique situation. And he was not just sharing niceties or patronizing sympathies. He shared with her profound spiritual truths that it appears he had not yet shared with anyone else. At that time, there was a great debate about which physical location was the appropriate place to worship God. Was it Mount Gerizim, as the Samaritans believed, or was it Jerusalem, as the Jews believed?

> Jesus said to this humble Samaritan woman, "'… You and your people will worship the Father neither on this mountain nor in Jerusalem… True worshippers will worship in spirit and truth. God is spirit, and it is necessary to worship God in spirit and truth.'" [17]

Animosity and conflict over the question of where to worship had waged for generations among the most distinguished religious scholars. And Jesus had an answer that totally reframed the debate. He essentially said that God is a spirit, and it does not matter the physical location where you worship, so long as you worship him in truth.

This was revolutionary teaching in a time when deities were so closely linked to temples and physical location. Yet, Jesus shared this most profound and revolutionary truth, not with the scholars that visited him, not when he spoke in the temple, not even in casual conversation with the devout who followed him. He revealed this truth to an apparently highly immoral person of second-class social status, from a race considered inferior, and a religion different from his own.

He shared a revolutionary new truth with someone who was an outcast among outcasts.

With Jesus, there were no "others." There were only people, individuals he treated with love and respect, no matter where they fit in society.

5

"*Christians Are Not Very Diverse*"
Choosing the Different

A visit to most modern churches is a study in sameness. In 2020, only 25% of Christian churches (Protestant and Catholic) were multiracial, meaning at least 20% of attendees were from minorities.[18] And this is a dramatic increase from 2012, when only 12% of churches were multiracial.[19] But churches are not just a bastion of racial sameness, they are also very likely to be composed of people from similar socioeconomic backgrounds. Only about half of evangelical Christians say they have a friend with a materially different household income or different level of education. Only about half have a friend of a different ethnicity.

This is to say nothing of politics, where in the 2016 presidential election about 80% of white evangelicals voted for one candidate, while 82% of black evangelicals voted for the other.[20]

This great sameness could be an active choice to be separate from people who are different. Or it could be the passive outcome of a series of choices made without diversity as a priority. But the net effect is that Christians, to the rest of the world, often appear to be isolated from those who are different.

But this homogeneity is not a reflection of how Jesus lived his life. The first-person accounts of the life and ministry of Jesus tell a much different story. Jesus lived humbly and simply and went out of his way to interact with all types of people. And, when choosing his closest disciples, the people he spent the most time with, he chose people with a remarkable diversity of backgrounds. Just consider the diversity of background among his twenty or so closest followers.

Peter was a fisherman who likely had no formal education or religious training. The first time he met with an assembly of senior Jewish leaders, they were "…caught by surprise by the confidence with which Peter and John spoke. After all, they understood that these apostles were uneducated and inexperienced…"[21] He was impetuous in both speech and action. On one occasion he said something so outlandish that Jesus literally looked at him and said, "Get away from me, Satan!"[22]

James and John were brothers from a family that was likely somewhat prominent. Their father Zebedee is mentioned on several occasions in the accounts of the life of Jesus, which suggests he had some degree of notoriety. John also mentions that he knew the high priest, which would have been unusual for an ordinary fisherman.[23] Jesus referred to both these men as "sons of thunder," suggesting they may have been prone to temper.[24]

Matthew was a tax collector, which in those days meant an agent of the Roman government. The Romans were an oppressive occupying force, and tax collectors were among their most visible representatives. In addition, tax collectors were notorious for extortion and hated for taking advantage of their own people.

Simon, another close follower, was called a "zealot." This was a term used to refer to a group of fanatical Jewish nationalists who were focused on trying to overthrow the Roman government. One can only imagine the awkward conversations he and Matthew must have had as they traveled together for several years.

Mary Magdalene played a prominent role in the life and ministry of Jesus, and she is identified as a woman from whom seven demons had been cast out.

> "Jesus traveled through the cities and villages, preaching and proclaiming the good news of God's kingdom. The Twelve were with him, along with some women who had been healed of evil spirits and sicknesses. Among them were Mary Magdalene (from whom seven demons had been thrown out)"[25]

Even if you are not someone who believes in demons, this definitely suggests she had a troubled past, likely dealing with severe mental or physical illness.

Joanna was the wife of the man who managed the household of the local king, Herod. She would have been wealthy, probably very polished, and well connected.[26] She was likely unaccustomed to spending time in close interaction with a coarse fisherman like Peter, or a political revolutionary like Simon.

Luke, who chronicled the life of Jesus and the early years of the Christian movement in great detail, was very well educated. Tradition holds he was a physician. Notably he was a gentile, which was most unusual in a movement that followed a Jewish rabbi and was heavily shaped by Jewish scripture.

This is not a group of people who likely would find themselves attending the same church in modern western Christian society. And, as different as these people seem today, in the Judea of two thousand years ago, differences among classes and between men and women were even more amplified. So, any diversity we might ascribe to this group is understated. Yet, for all their dramatic differences, they had something in common that was even more powerful. They sought the same truth, believed in the same God that loved all humankind.

Jesus himself traveled across Canaan and surrounding areas, to people of different tribes and ethnicities. When he was a child, his family lived briefly in Egypt. During his ministry he visited the homeland of the hated Samaritans, visited people of completely different races and religious traditions in what is now Syria and Jordan. One of his most enduring commands to his followers was to go to all nations.

Jesus surrounded himself with diversity of background, personality, and opinion. He moved well outside the cultural comfort zone for someone raised as a tradesman in a small Jewish town. Thousands of years before even the most progressive civilizations became enlightened enough to value diversity, Jesus modeled exactly that.

The diversity of this group surely played a significant role in the spread of the teachings of Jesus both during his life and afterwards. Among his followers were people who could understand and communicate with people from virtually any walk of life, and any background. Over the next few decades this group would crisscross the earth in places as far away as Rome, Ethiopia, Persia, and India. They would speak to handicapped beggars on the street and kings and religious leaders of all flavors. This group of people who knew Jesus personally had an impact that still echoes in every corner of the world two thousand years later.

Diversity was not a missed opportunity or an accidental byproduct. It was an intentional choice and a critical contributor to the incredible impact Jesus had on the world. Jesus sought a kind of unity, not born of everyone trying to be the same, but of many different kinds of people following the same truth. Many different kinds of sheep, all following the same shepherd.

> Jesus said, "I am the good shepherd. I know my own sheep and they know me. I have other sheep that don't belong to this sheep pen. I must lead them, too. They will listen to my voice and there will be one flock, with one shepherd."[27]

6

"*Christians Are So Angry*"
Part 1: When Jesus Chose Anger

"[Christians] are angry at many things… 'sins'… especially anything of a sexual nature. Christians fight against anything that smacks of homosexuality or gender identity…. Even the hint of not believing in banning every abortion will stir up the kind of anger that leads to war…. Many Christians also get angry over anything that even comes close to taking away freedom or rights. Don't dare suggest I wear a mask or get vaccinated because it might contribute to reducing the spread of a deadly virus. Freedom to carry guns is also a sacred right that causes many Christians to be angry when it is threatened…"[28]

– *Post from Medium.com*

> *"The spell of Christianity can stunt emotional growth and allow bitter behavior and emotions to flourish. Judgment becomes a daily habit. With judgment comes bitter reaction, which becomes habit. Suddenly everyone's a sinner and should be treated like such. This is where the habit of anger comes in. It stems from the error of trying to control someone or something outside yourself..."[29]*
>
> *– Post from Quora.com*

To the rest of the world, Christians often seem angry. Angry at those who see the world differently, angry at those who disagree, angry at those who do not understand, even angry at those who do not believe the same things. For many people, the word "Christian" immediately brings to mind a protest sign, an angry post on social media, or even a frustrating conversation.

Of course, there are many times when anger seems to be a perfectly appropriate emotion. We live in an imperfect world, with no shortage of injustice and suffering, so there are certainly times anger is understandable, even desirable as a catalyst for change. One of the early followers of Jesus, Paul of Tarsus, famously wrote in a letter to other Christ followers that they should "be angry without sinning."[30]

So, this begs the question, did Jesus ever get angry? And if he did, what made him angry?

On one occasion, Jesus met a man with a deformed hand and wanted to heal him. But it was the sabbath day. The Jewish people believed the Sabbath, the first day of each week, had been set aside by God as a day of rest. But, over hundreds of years, this simple rule, "Rest on the first day of the week," had been complicated by scores of rules about what was and was not rest, and intricate definitions of work.

So, when Jesus spoke to this man about his hand, the teachers of the religious law were watching him closely, trying to trap him into breaking a rule. Mark, an early follower of Jesus who documented the first person accounts of Peter, described the events as follows:

> "Jesus returned to the synagogue. A man with a withered hand was there. Wanting to bring charges against Jesus, [religious leaders] were watching Jesus closely to see if he would heal on the Sabbath. He said to the man with the withered hand, "Step up where people can see you." Then he said to them, "Is it legal on the Sabbath to do good or to do evil, to save life or to kill?" But they said nothing. Looking around at them with anger, deeply grieved at their unyielding hearts, [Jesus] said to the man, "Stretch out your hand." So he did, and his hand was made healthy."[31]

Yes, Jesus became angry. He looked at the religious leaders "with anger, deeply grieved." But his anger was directed at those who used religious power and religious rules to avoid helping someone who needed help. He was angry at those who put religion ahead of people.

Perhaps the most dramatic example of Jesus being angry was when he drove out merchants who had set up shop in the temple. In those days, each citizen would visit the temple at least once a year, to offer a sacrifice and reconnect with God. Many would travel for days or weeks to get there. Most were not wealthy and would save up what little they had for the journey and an offering to give at the temple.

However, the temple would not accept the standard Roman coins that everyone used. These coins included an image of Caesar and were considered idols. So, the coins had to be exchanged for a different currency that would be accepted by the temple. Money changers would set up in the temple to exchange the coins, but these people were notorious for taking advantage of the poor rural pilgrims who did not understand the appropriate exchange rates. Also, merchants would sell animals that the temple deemed appropriate for sacrifice, often at exorbitant prices. One can imagine the noise and chaos of animals and people clamoring, the pervasive stress of rural folks navigating a crowded, complex, and unfamiliar place, everyone on guard with their hands on their wallets.[32][33]

This was not a great environment for people to be at ease and draw close to God. For Jesus, who had a deep passion for making it easy for people to connect with God, the sight of all this happening right in the temple made him angry. John, a follower of Jesus who was there, described what happened this way:

"It was nearly time for the Jewish Passover, and Jesus went up to Jerusalem. He found in the temple those who were selling cattle, sheep, and doves, as well as those involved in exchanging currency sitting there. He made a whip from ropes and chased them all out of the temple, including the cattle and the sheep. He scattered the coins and overturned the tables of those who exchanged currency. He said to the dove sellers, 'Get these things out of here! Don't make my Father's house a place of business.'"[34]

Matthew, another follower of Jesus, said that, as this was happening, Jesus said, "'It's written, "My house will be called a house of prayer." But you've made it a hideout for crooks.'"[35]

Again, Jesus directed his anger not at sinners who needed help, but at people who used religion as an opportunity to take advantage of people. In this case, he was focused on people who preyed on the fears and ignorance of others for financial gain. The temple should be first and foremost a "house of prayer," a place for people to connect with God. Anything that got in the way of that was unacceptable.

This is a repeating pattern in the life of Jesus. He embraced sinners and outcasts and marginalized people, treating them with kindness and patience. On the few occasions he showed anger, that anger was not directed at those who sinned. Rather, he reserved his anger for the religious establishment that used the name of God but did not actually point people to God, who used religion as a cloak to make themselves feel superior instead of showing the way to God. Jesus directed his anger at the religious system of his day, the leaders who used rules and customs to create distance between God and man. Jesus was angry when people put religion ahead of people, customs and traditions ahead of meeting real tangible needs.

Below is an excerpt from a particularly heated conversation between Jesus and religious teachers. It provides a good example of how Jesus viewed the religion of his day.

> "'How terrible it will be for you legal experts and Pharisees! Hypocrites! You shut people out of the kingdom of heaven. You don't enter yourselves, and you won't allow those who want to enter to do so.
>
> "'How terrible it will be for you legal experts and Pharisees! Hypocrites! You give to God a tenth... but you forget about the more important matters of the Law: justice, peace, and faith. You ought to give a tenth but without forgetting about those more important matters. You blind guides! You filter out an ant but swallow a camel.
>
> "'How terrible it will be for you legal experts and Pharisees! Hypocrites! You clean the outside of the cup and plate, but inside they are full of violence and pleasure seeking.

> "'How terrible it will be for you legal experts and Pharisees! Hypocrites! You are like whitewashed tombs. They look beautiful on the outside. But inside they are full of dead bones and all kinds of filth. In the same way, you look righteous to people. But inside you are full of pretense and rebellion.'"[36]

If Jesus walked the earth today, it seems very unlikely he would be heard shouting angrily at those who do not believe, or who the church calls "sinners." There is little to suggest he would engage in angry social media exchanges with ordinary imperfect people trying to find their way or asking honest questions. Based on what we know about the life of Jesus, it is far more likely he would direct his anger at the religious folks who use his name without embracing his true mission.

7

"Christians Are So Angry"
Part 2: When Jesus Said No to Anger

Jesus occasionally showed anger when he encountered people in power, especially religious people, who oppressed or took advantage of people. But, although Jesus sometimes became angry at the mistreatment of others, when Jesus was attacked personally, he responded with calm grace. One of Jesus' most famous quotes on the subject of conflict is this:

> "'You have heard that it was said, "An eye for an eye and a tooth for a tooth." But I say to you that you must not oppose those who want to hurt you. If people slap you on your right cheek, you must turn the left cheek to them as well.'"[37]

Jesus lived his life with extreme humility, and did not view a personal affront, no matter how egregious, as a justification for anger. On one occasion, Jesus was traveling to Jerusalem and the shortest path was through Samaria.

Luke's account of the journey says, "...But the Samaritan villagers refused to welcome him because he was determined to go to Jerusalem. When the disciples James and John saw this, they said, 'Lord, do you want us to call fire down from heaven to consume them?' But Jesus turned and spoke sternly to them, and they went on to another village."[38]

As we discussed earlier, Samaritans and Jews had a deep religious and ethnic bigotry toward each other. Yet, Jesus, although a Jewish teacher, had embraced the Samaritans. He even made a Samaritan the star of one of his most famous parables, about a person helping someone in need.[39] Yet, even so, the Samaritans rejected Jesus. They did not want him in their village. They repaid his love and outreach with bigotry and rejection. It is normal, many would say even appropriate, to become angry when met with rejection. The disciples of Jesus certainly responded this way, even suggesting that fire be called down from heaven as judgment on those who rejected them.

But Jesus did not get angry, and even admonished his disciples not to get angry. He just turned and went to another place.

There are other such instances from the life of Jesus when he showed this kind of humility in the face of a personal attack. But perhaps the most compelling example is near the end of his life. He was arrested on trumped up charges by religious leaders. They presented him to the local Roman authorities, Herod and Pontius Pilate, and asked that Jesus be executed for his supposed crimes. It was a profound injustice, a horrible repayment of evil for good.

"[Pontius Pilate] said to them, 'You brought this man before me as one who was misleading the people. I have questioned him in your presence and found nothing in this man's conduct that provides a legal basis for the charges you have brought against him. Neither did Herod, because Herod returned him to us. He's done nothing that deserves death.'

But with one voice they shouted, 'Away with this man! Release Barabbas to us.' They kept shouting out, 'Crucify him! Crucify him!' For the third time, Pilate said to them, 'Why? What wrong has he done? I've found no legal basis for the death penalty in his case. Therefore, I will have him whipped, then let him go.' But they were adamant, shouting their demand that Jesus be crucified. Their voices won out. Pilate issued his decision to grant their request. When they arrived at the place called The Skull, they crucified him, along with the criminals..."[40]

After a life spent helping people, teaching and healing, Jesus was sentenced to death in that same community. The life and person of Jesus has been studied perhaps more than any other, by people of all faiths. Yet, no one has made a case that Jesus deserved to die. Even the secular leaders of his day found no fault in Jesus. In fact, it is nearly impossible to find anyone who claims Jesus did anything wrong at all. Christians believe Jesus never sinned. Yet he was sentenced to a brutal and publicly humiliating execution. It was the ultimate injustice.

So, in the face of this most extreme injustice, how did Jesus respond? He did the same thing he had done throughout his life, he stayed grounded in his mission. He was on earth to lead people to God, sharing the heart of God was everything to him. He put others first. He counted any offense to himself as nothing. With that in mind, the last words of Jesus as documented by Luke are stunning. As Jesus hung on the cross, unjustly convicted, his body brutalized and naked, slowly dying in public, he looked at the crowd of people around them and said these words:

> "'Father, forgive them, for they don't know what they're doing.'"[41]

So many modern Christians bristle at every affront, lash out at those who disagree or offend. Conflicting ideas, attitudes, or beliefs are often met with smug withdrawal, defensiveness, or outright aggression. And sometimes there are very real attacks on Christians, be they direct or subtle. But, while responding to an attack with anger is understandable, maybe even natural, that is not how Jesus responded. No Christian today is attacked like Jesus was, yet he responded with love.

> On one occasion Jesus amazed people when he said, "'You have heard that it was said, "You must love your neighbor and hate your enemy." But I say to you, love your enemies and pray for those who harass you.'"[42]

Anger is easy, anger is natural. Love is hard. Yet, with Jesus, love was not reserved for those who agreed with him, and anger was not deployed for personal defense. In the face of personal injustice and even outright attack, Jesus did not choose anger. He always chose love.

8

"Christians Just Want Political Power"
A Different Kind of Kingdom

"Less than half of evangelical Christians (42%) say they have expressed public disapproval of political allies for using what respondents recognized as unacceptable words or actions. Around a quarter (26%) say they tend to believe insulting personal remarks made by political leaders who share their ideology toward opponents are justified."

– *Lifeway Research*

"...When the world is greedy, you are generous. When the world is cruel, you are kind. When the world is fearful, you are faithful. When the world is proud,

> *you are humble. How do you know we're Christian? By our love. Yes, we say. Yes to all of this. Right until the moment when we think that our kindness, our faithfulness, or our humility carries with it a concrete political cost. We think we know what's just, and we can't do justice without power... And so, in our arrogance, we think we know better than God. We can't let kindness or humility stand in the way of justice. Yet we're sowing the wind, and now we reap the whirlwind. The world's most-Christian advanced nation is tearing itself apart, and its millions of believers bear much of the blame."[43]*
>
> – David French

Before Jesus began his earthly ministry in earnest, he spent some time in the wilderness alone. During this time, he faced a series of temptations. Christians believe these temptations were tests to demonstrate the heart of Jesus, to show whether his motivations were a match for the incredible life he was going to lead. His responses to these temptations were meant as a model for how his followers should respond in the face of similar situations.

The second of these temptations is described by Luke as follows:

> "Next the devil led him to a high place and showed him in a single instant all the kingdoms of the world. The devil said, 'I will give you this whole domain and the glory of all these kingdoms. It's

been entrusted to me and I can give it to anyone I want. Therefore, if you will worship me, it will all be yours.'"[44]

Whether you believe in the devil or not, or whether this was a literal event or a parable, this was a story relayed by Jesus himself. Clearly, he intended to make a point by sharing it, to share a window into how he felt his followers should respond in similar situations.

In this recounting, Jesus was being offered an opportunity to rule as a king. In other words, he was offered unlimited political power over the entire world. Jesus had come to change the world. How better to do that than by ruling the world? Jesus had very clear views about justice, right and wrong, and how people should relate to God and to others. If he were the political ruler of the world, he would have incredible leverage to create laws and impact society to implement his vision. In this story, it almost seems like Jesus is being handed the perfect tool to accomplish his mission.

But Jesus said no to political power.

A few years later, at the peak of his popularity, it was the people around Jesus who offered him political power. John, a close friend of Jesus, writes:

> "[He] understood that they were about to come and force him to be their king, so he took refuge again, alone on a mountain."[45]

Again, Jesus said no to political power. Why? Surely achieving great power in society would be an excellent way to change society. Why would a man who wants to change the world turn down the power to change the world?

Jesus was focused on building something so great that even the greatest political power would seem trivial by comparison. By that point in history, the great empires of Egypt, Babylon, Alexander the Great's Greece, and others had all risen to unmatched power and then dissolved into history. They all exerted their will on the world for a season and then faded. Each one polarized the world into enemies and friends, conquerors and the conquered. In the time of Jesus, Rome was the dominant political power, perhaps more powerful than any empire in history. Yet even at the peak of its power the seeds of its demise were being sown. Political power is inherently transient and divisive. It is a zero-sum game where there is always a winner and a loser, and every victory plants the seeds for the next revolution.

Jesus was playing a different game, a longer game, wielding a far greater kind of influence. Jesus knew that real change comes from the inside out, not the outside in.

> "'...Out of your heart come evil thoughts, murder, unfaithfulness,... vulgar deeds, stealing, telling lies, and insulting others.'"[46]

Jesus was not looking to use governmental power or cultural pressure to force people to change their actions. He wanted to change the world by changing hearts, to rewire our world view by teaching us to view each person through the lens of love.

> "Jesus answered: 'Love... God with all your heart, soul, and mind... Love others as much as you love yourself. All the Law.... [is] based on these two.'"[47]

Jesus wanted to connect each human with their neighbor and connect all humans to God. That is a goal infinitely greater, more challenging, and more important than achieving any level of political power.

And, if changing hearts is the goal, political power is simply not the best tool for the job. A person's heart and motivation does not change simply because they are forced to change their behavior. Jesus was building a movement, a way of viewing each other and God, which would outlast any governmental authority. His message was more significant and broader than any political policy. Aligning himself with a government would weaken his message, not strengthen it.

This truth has significant implications in our modern political environment. Of course, Christians should vote and should have informed opinions on political issues. But it is dangerous to draw a direct link between political identity and faith identity, to say being a Christian means you must support one particular political party or political position.

Political parties and political movements are human institutions, founded and managed by imperfect people torn between their own self-interest and the greater good. People are not so wise as to know exactly the will of God on each specific political issue. Politicians are not so perfect that they can be trusted to always act in the will of God. And God is not so weak that he can only accomplish his will through one organization.

Yet, many Christians invoke the name of Jesus to further their chosen political cause. In many cases, issues that seem well beyond the clear direction of scripture are treated with moral fervor. Is there really an appropriate Christian position on the number of immigrants admitted to the U.S. each year? Would Jesus have clear direction on the percentage tax rate for each tax bracket? Is the message of Jesus advanced further if infrastructure spending is twenty percent higher or lower? There are moral aspects to these and many other issues, but can we confidently say what position Jesus would take, if he took one at all?

> One on occasion, local leaders tried to engage Jesus in a debate about taxes. "'Teacher,' they said, '...We know how honest you are. You teach the way of God truthfully... Is it right to pay taxes to Caesar or not?'
>
> "Jesus said, 'Here, show me the coin used for the tax.' When they handed him a Roman coin, he asked, 'Whose picture and title are stamped on it?'
>
> "'Caesar's,' they replied.
>
> "'Well, then,' he said, 'give to Caesar what belongs to Caesar, and give to God what belongs to God.' His reply amazed them, and they went away."[48]

Jesus simply refused to lend the weight of God to a political debate. He was focused on something bigger.

Putting the name of Christ on a single political policy or organization is at best folly, and at worst an idolatry that undermines the message of Jesus. When we do this, I fear Christians weaken our ability to further the true mission of Jesus. I suspect that when many non-believers think of Christianity, they see a likely political adversary rather than someone who will demonstrate the unconditional love of God. How many times do we see prominent Christians in the news talking about a political candidate, a cultural concern, or a political issue, and how rarely do we see them talking about Jesus? Has the core of Christianity become a cause or a political movement rather than Christ? Have we taken the bait? Have we failed the second temptation?

Regardless of where you stand on the abortion issue, the overturning of Roe vs Wade provides a great illustration. In 2022, the Supreme Court overturned Roe vs Wade, which opened the door to waves of new restrictions on abortion. Many Christians fought for years to accomplish this, believing abortion is a sin against God akin to murder. Over the decades, Christians have at times voted for people they knew were otherwise immoral because the candidate promised to help overturn abortion. They have demonized women they knew needed love because they wanted to take a firm stance on abortion. In some cases, Christians have knowingly or unknowingly fought policies that provide care for crisis pregnancies and women in need, because they wanted to avoid any shadow of support for abortion.

After so much sacrifice and work over so many decades, you might have expected incredible jubilation among Christians writ large when the Supreme Court overturned Roe. But repeatedly when I spoke with Christians about the case, or read responses from Christians online, the feeling was so much more muted. There was not widespread jubilation. Some even felt a kind of heaviness.

Perhaps it was an acknowledgment of the incredible cost and compromise it took to get this particular political result. Or perhaps it was the knowledge that, as powerful as this legal change was, it did not change one single heart. Not one person suddenly decided abortion was wrong because the Supreme Court changed the law. Not one heart suddenly turned closer to God. There was not a flood of people walking into Christian churches wanting to know more about this wonderful God in whose name this court decision was made.

Politics responds to the problems of the world by imposing laws and policies that change people's behavior. Jesus taught us to respond to the problems of the world by showing people the kind of love that changes hearts. Laws change actions, but laws cannot change hearts. Jesus did not advocate for changes to laws or government; he never made a protest sign or backed a political leader. Instead, he went out of his way to understand people and their context, to show everyone unconditional love. Jesus fought for hearts, not for causes.

> Napoleon Bonaparte said, "I know men and I tell you that Jesus Christ is no mere man. Between Him

and every other person in the world there is no possible term of comparison. Alexander, Caesar, Charlemagne, and I have founded empires. But on what did we rest the creation of our genius? Upon force. Jesus Christ founded His empire upon love; and at this hour millions of men would die for Him."[49]

Genuinely loving people is so much more difficult than conquering them. Demonstrating unconditional love to others is harder than playing politics. So hard in fact, you might say it is impossible for a human to love that way. You might say that kind of love provides evidence of a higher power. You would probably say that kind of love draws people like nothing else can. And through that lens, the ability to rise above politics, to put faith and love above earthly power, is a great testimony. It accomplishes what politics never can.

Sharing the love of God provides a legacy that lasts far longer than any candidate or political issue of the day. Perhaps that is why Jesus always said no to the pursuit of earthly power. It was an inferior tool for the job he wanted to do. Jesus wanted to change the world by changing hearts. And love was the only thing powerful enough to accomplish that mission.

9

"Christians Don't Like Gay People"
Knowing and Loving

"My choices, it seemed, were to be branded a sinner and live my life alone; to abandon my faith, the one thing I held most dear in the entire world; or to lie to everyone, pretend I was straight, and forget about it all."[50]

—*Justin Lee*

Over the past couple of decades in the U.S., LGBTQ rights have become more of a mainstream issue. In parallel, many Christians have become more visible and outspoken in their opposition to people being openly LGBTQ in mainstream culture. Christians have lined up against gay marriage, insurance benefits for gay couples, the ability for gay couples to adopt, transgender people playing sports, even the idea of having separate bathrooms not designated for a specific gender. Listen to a Christian speak about these issues and you most often hear frustration, anger, even fear. Those in non-Christian world, both gay and straight, are often left with the impression that Christians simply do not like, even hate, people who are not traditional heterosexuals.

To explain their views on homosexuality, Christians often point to seven specific passages, three from the Torah and four from the letters Paul of Tarsus wrote to Christian churches in the first century.[51] The standard English translation of these passages does not leave much room for ambiguity.[52] [53] But some argue that an understanding the historical context in which these passages were written and reviewing the original Hebrew or Greek wording opens up questions as to their intent.[54]

> For instance, the original Law of Moses as recorded in Leviticus within the Torah states: "You must not give any of your children to offer them over to Molech so that you do not defile your God's name: I am the LORD. You must not have sexual intercourse with a man as you would with a woman; it is a detestable practice. You will not have sexual relations with any animal, becoming unclean by it. Nor will a woman present herself before an animal to mate with it; it is a perversion. Do not make yourselves unclean in any of these ways because that is how the nations that I am throwing out before you became unclean."[55]

Most Christians believe this scripture condemns homosexuality. But some point out that this passage is about worshipping other gods and is included in a list of rituals associated with the worship of the god Molech, such sacrificing children, forced prostitution of males, and bestiality. So, some suggest perhaps this part of the law is not about homosexual behavior, but about worshipping other gods.[56]

Another example of a passage interpreted to understand homosexuality is found in Paul's letter to an early Christian church. He writes:

> "They exchanged the glory of the immortal God for images that look like mortal humans: birds, animals, and reptiles. So, God abandoned them to their hearts' desires, which led to the moral corruption of degrading their own bodies with each other. They traded God's truth for a lie, and they worshiped and served the creation instead of the creator, who is blessed forever. Amen. That's why God abandoned them to degrading lust. Their females traded natural sexual relations for unnatural sexual relations. Also, in the same way, the males traded natural sexual relations with females, and burned with lust for each other. Males performed shameful actions with males, and they were paid back with the penalty they deserved for their mistake in their own bodies."[57]

Some point out this passage references homosexuality in the

context of a discussion of idolatry, and that homosexual sex was a common ritual in the worship of Greek, Roman, and pagan gods in those days. So, there is a possibility this passage was, much like the passage from Leviticus above, really about idol worship. Others argue that the term "natural" above refers to each person's innate natural sexual desires, not some broader law of nature. This would open the door for sexual behavior that is aligned with who God naturally created you to be. But the counter argument dismisses this as overlaying modern concepts of innate sexuality onto something that was written centuries before the concept of innate sexual orientation was understood.

But in these pages, our focus is not to analyze the writings of Paul of Tarsus or ancient Hebrew law. Our goal is to understand the person of Jesus as it relates to these issues. So, what did he, the Christ that Christians follow, have to say about gay people? The short answer is nothing. Of all the first-person accounts of Jesus life, and chronicles of the things he said, there is no mention of homosexuality. Jesus would have encountered gay people and, given his remarkable ability to understand people, sexual orientation would not have escaped his notice. We can only speculate as to why Jesus never discussed homosexuality, or why whatever he said was not recorded. But, if we want to understand whether Jesus would have interacted LGBTQ people like modern Christians do, there is enough information to make an informed estimate.

First, we know that Jesus was supportive of committed, monogamous relationships.

"Jesus answered, 'Haven't you read that at the beginning the creator made them male and female? And God said, "Because of this a man should leave his father and mother and be joined together with his wife, and the two will be one flesh." So, they are no longer two but one flesh. Therefore, humans must not pull apart what God has put together.'"[58]

Jesus' view of marriage was a radically selfless commitment, two people so dedicated to each other that they functioned as one being. Some scholars point to this verse as proof that Jesus taught marriage was only between a biological man and a biological woman. Others claim "male" and "female" just refer to two halves of the marital unit, and that the "two become one flesh" phrase speaks to a level of equality that makes the distinction between two people irrelevant.

But as much as Jesus supported marriage, he highlighted that it was not for everyone. He even taught that some men are born without the desire for marriage, and presumably for sexual intercourse.

"[Jesus] said to them, 'Not everyone grasps this teaching, only those for whom it is meant. For there are different reasons why men do not marry – some because they were born without the desire, some because they have been castrated, and some because they have renounced marriage for the sake of the Kingdom of Heaven. Whoever can grasp this, let him do so.'"[59]

Jesus also taught that the whole idea of marriage and gender was something of a temporary construct for this mortal life but would not endure in eternity.

> "'Teacher, Moses said If a man who doesn't have children dies, his brother must marry his wife and produce children for his brother. Now there were seven brothers among us. The first one married, then died. Because he had no children, he left his widow to his brother. The same thing happened with the second brother and the third, and in fact with all seven brothers. Finally, the woman died. At the resurrection, which of the seven brothers will be her husband? They were all married to her.' Jesus responded, 'You are wrong because you don't know either the scriptures or God's power. At the resurrection, people won't marry nor will they be given in marriage. Instead, they will be like angels from God.' Now when the crowd heard this, they were astonished at his teaching."[60]

This means that there is a life after this one, an eternity that makes these few years on earth seem impossibly small. And in that eternity, there is no marriage. And the phrase, "they will be like angels," in this context suggests that in eternity there will be no gender as we think of it.

When faced with questions about human marriage and sexuality, Jesus responded as he so often did with other issues, by disrupting assumptions and zooming out to a larger truth. Marriage is not just a social and legal arrangement; it is a radical mutual commitment that leads to two people becoming one. Some people do not have the desire for sexual relationship and marriage, and that is okay. And marriage is a temporary construct for this life and does not exist in eternity. Those are some disruptive truths today; it is impossible to overstate how revolutionary they were in the culture of first-century Palestine. No wonder Matthew pointed out, "...When the crowd heard this, they were astonished at his teaching."[61]

While Jesus' teaching on human marriage and sexuality challenged and surprised his audience, he never addressed the question of homosexuality directly. Even those who feel confident in their interpretation of the broader scriptures on this topic may still have at least a small bit of uncertainty. There is nothing wrong with that, of course. Uncertainty can be a sign of faithful, open-minded study.

But this uncertainty might raise a big question in the minds of Christians. "If I do not know for sure whether homosexuality is right or wrong, how do I know how to treat these people?" Based on what we know about the life and teachings of Jesus, I'm not sure that question really matters at all.

Jesus taught that we should love every person. He commanded his followers not to judge others. He taught that we should resist the urge to sort people into buckets according to who was right and who was wrong. Jesus frequently spent time with those that religious society considered to be in the wrong, sinners of all types. Even if a Christian interprets scripture in a way that suggests LBGTQ people are in the wrong, there is nothing in the teaching of Jesus that gives Christians the license to treat these individuals differently.

To be Christ-like, a Christian's every interaction with an LBGTQ person should come from a place of selfless love. But many Christians do not interact with LGBTQ people directly. So, the only exposure this community has to Christians is through the public stance the Christian community takes on issues the LGBTQ community cares about. The list of these positions held by Christians reads like a series of gut punches to the soul.

> The love you feel for your committed life partner is wrong and evil.
>
> The government should pass laws that say your relationship cannot be recognized.
>
> You should not be able to share a life insurance plan with your chosen family.
>
> You should not get to choose which bathroom you use.
>
> You should not be able to have children.

In the heat of the culture wars and the politicization of everything, it is easy to forget that behind every LGBTQ issue are LGBTQ people, individual human beings God knows completely and loves completely. Those people are more important to God than any issue. Even if one believes there is political and theological justification and merit behind each of these positions, is shouting these points really the purest expression of how Christ would interact with this community?

Said another way, if Jesus had a moment of attention from this community, would he spend that time reciting and explaining his position on whether same sex couples should share an insurance plan? Would Jesus stand in the public square and make impassioned arguments about bathroom choices in the name of God? Given only a moment to speak to them, what would he say? Of course, we do not know for sure, but based on what we know about his words and actions, I think he would say something like this:

> I see you completely.
> I know you completely.
> I love you completely.
> Follow me.

10

"Christians Want To Take Away Reproductive Rights"
The Humility of Not Knowing Everything

"While the Roman Catholic Church is an outspoken critic of abortion, U.S. Catholics were divided on the issue in the 2014 survey, with 48% supportive of legal abortion and 47% opposed... Indeed, among all those who are part of the evangelical tradition, nearly twice as many say they oppose legal abortion as support it (63% to 33%)... By comparison, only 35% of those who are part of the mainline Protestant tradition say abortion should be illegal in all or most cases, with 60% in support of keeping abortion legal." [62]

– Pew Research 2018

The legality and morality of abortion has been one of most divisive issues in the U.S. over the past several decades, and that debate has also raged among Christians. But, while a significant percentage of Christians believe abortion should be legal, vocal opposition to abortion has become one of the most publicly visible messages of Christianity.

For many Christian denominations, especially those who are more evangelical or fundamentalist, the belief that abortion is akin to murder has become a core Christian belief, almost to the same degree as the existence of God and the resurrection of Jesus. As the importance of this issue has grown in Christian circles, Christians have used a desire to end abortion as justification for a whole host of activities. Some have been relatively peaceful and helpful, like starting organizations to help women find ways to keep and care for their children, supporting adoption agencies that find homes for babies whose parents cannot care for them, or engaging in good faith discussions around how to balance the needs and rights of women with the rights of their unborn babies.

But all too often, Christians have used views on abortion to justify words and behavior that seem, at a minimum ungracious, and sometimes outright hateful. Abortion clinics have been bombed in the name of Christ. People protesting in abortion clinic parking lots have screamed hateful things at pregnant teenagers in the name of Christ. People have voted for leaders who are overtly immoral and do not reflect the values of Christ, based solely on the fact they oppose abortion. Christians have demonized and judged women facing incredibly difficult situations instead of embracing them. To the outside world, the Christian crusade against abortion might seem fueled by hatred for those who disagree rather than a mission of love to protect unborn life.

In the time of Jesus, abortion was practiced throughout the Roman Empire and likely the world. The techniques were unreliable and not terribly sophisticated, but there was a range of herbs that were known to abort pregnancy. Silphium, rue, and birthwort were common means of inducing abortion in Greco-Roman times. The Roman government had no prohibitions against abortion. However there does seem to have been some objection to abortions that occurred after the fetus had functioning senses. Aristotle acknowledge this principle, as well as the inherent difficulty in determining the moment life begins when he wrote:

> "...let abortion be procured before sense and life have begun; what may or may not be lawfully done in these cases depends on the question of life and sensation."[63]

The Hebrew law of the day, originally passed down from Moses a few thousand years earlier, addressed abortion only briefly and discussed a narrow set of situations. Jesus would certainly have been aware of abortion, but we have no record of him ever speaking on the topic. So, we can only infer how Jesus might have viewed the abortion issue based on what we know about his values and actions.

Generally, a person's position on abortion can be described with answers to the following three questions:

1. Is human life valuable?
2. When does human life begin?
3. What other values can outweigh the value of that life?

Inferring Jesus' thoughts on the first question is simple. Jesus said that God sees all life, knowing even when a small animal dies.

> "'Aren't two sparrows sold for a small coin? But not one of them will fall to the ground without your Father knowing about it already. Even the hairs of your head are all counted. Don't be afraid. You are worth more than many sparrows.'"[64]

And Jesus made a point on several occasions to emphasize the value of children's lives in particular. In that society, children had no status, often no rights, viewed as little more than property. But Jesus disagreed.

> On one occasion we find, "...Some people brought children to Jesus so that he would place his hands on them and pray. But the disciples scolded them. 'Allow the children to come to me,' Jesus said. 'Don't forbid them, because the kingdom of heaven belongs to people like these children.'"[65]

So, if human life is valuable, especially the life of a child, the next question must be: "When does human life begin?" This is perhaps the most critical question and provides the foundational context for any discussion about abortion. The position fervently supported by many Christians says a fertilized human embryo in the mother's womb is just as much a human being as a four-year-old child playing in the park. Most people, Christian or not, would say there is no justification for killing an innocent four-year-old, and just about any action is justifiable to save that child's life. This assumption underlies the "win at all costs" mentality many Christians have toward the abortion issue.

But in the time of Jesus, as throughout much of history, there have been a wide range of views on when life begins. Some say at the time of conception, others at the moment the limbs are formed, the moment the heart starts beating, the moment the brain is formed, the moment of first movement, when the child can survive on its own outside the womb, or even the moment a child breathes on its own outside its mother. Until the late nineteenth and early twentieth centuries, many Christian religions including the Roman Catholic Church, permitted abortions early in pregnancies on the basis that the child was not alive until the moment of "quickening." Quickening was the point at which the fetus was assumed to be alive, usually sometime during the first trimester.[66]

There is no record of Jesus directly addressing the question of when life begins. There are some references to the beginning of life in the Hebrew law and prophets, which was the prevailing religious canon of Jesus' day. These passages have been used by modern-day Christians to make a case for when a fetus becomes a living soul. Those who believe life begins at conception often point to the following passages:

> "You are the one who created my innermost parts; you knit me together while I was still in my mother's womb... Your eyes saw my embryo, and on your scroll every day was written that was being formed for me, before any one of them had yet happened."[67]
>
> "Before I formed you in the womb, I knew you; before you were born, I separated you for myself..."[68]

Both make the point that God knows us before we are born, and that he creates us as unique beings for a unique purpose. But while these passages definitely say God sees us and relates to us before we are born, it stops short of saying whether we are a living spirit at the moment of conception or some point later in the developmental process. The passage from Jeremiah above was originally written in Hebrew, and the word translated as 'formed' was a word often used to describe the process of a potter forming clay. It is the same word used in the book of Genesis to describe the moment humankind became sentient.

> "...The LORD God formed the human from the topsoil of the fertile land and blew life's breath into his nostrils. The human came to life."[69]

The "forming" came first and then the human came alive. God formed Adam, but he was not a living soul until God breathed life into him. If we assume the word "form" had the same meaning in the passage from Jerimiah as it did in Genesis, you could infer that a child's body is formed in the womb before it becomes truly a living spirit. In other words, the process of forming a body is separate from the process of it being truly living spirit. This would open the door for the possibility there is a portion of pregnancy where the embryo or fetus is not spiritually alive.

Another passage that has been used on both sides of the abortion argument is the following from the Law of Moses:

> "If people are fighting with each other and happen to hurt a pregnant woman so badly that her unborn child dies, then, even if no other harm follows, he must be fined. He must pay the amount set by the woman's husband and confirmed by judges. But if any harm follows, then you are to give life for life."[70]

This clearly implies that an unborn child has value and causing a miscarriage against a woman's will is a crime. However, the law explicitly states that the penalty for killing an unborn child is a fine, whereas the penalty for taking the life of the mother would be the death penalty. This suggests the Law of Moses places a different value on the life of a fetus than the life of someone who has already been born.

When we move past the question of exactly when life begins, we must also consider whether there is anything that might outweigh the value of that life. We live in an imperfect world. Sometimes terrible things happen that require us to make difficult decisions. Is there any situation that would justify ending a pregnancy? Again, the Hebrew canon used in the time of Jesus did not provide much detail on this topic. The only mention of abortion is this passage from the book of Numbers, which describes abortion being administered if a woman becomes pregnant while having an affair.

> "...A man may suspect that his wife has had an affair and has broken faith with him, then the man will bring his wife to the priest... The priest will make the woman stand before the LORD... The water of bitterness that brings the curse will be in the hands of the priest. Then the priest will make her swear a solemn pledge, saying to the woman, 'If no man has slept with you and if you haven't had an affair, becoming defiled while married to your husband, then be immune from the water of bitterness that brings these curses. But if you have had an affair while married to your husband, if you have defiled yourself, and a man other than your husband has had intercourse with you.... may the water that brings these curses enter your stomach and make your womb discharge and make you miscarry.' And the woman will say, 'I agree, I agree.' When he has made her drink the water, if she has defiled herself and has broken faith with her husband, then the water that brings the curse will enter her, causing bitterness, and her womb will discharge and she will miscarry."[71]

Modern Christians can justifiably debate whether conceiving a baby as the result of an affair is sufficient justification for an abortion. But we cannot use the Hebrew law as justification for prohibiting abortion without also acknowledging that same law suggested there were some situations so unfortunate that ending a pregnancy was justified.

Of course, there are situations where a pregnancy has much greater consequences than a woman bearing a child conceived as the result of an extramarital affair. There are cases where the continued development of a fetus threatens the life of the woman carrying it. In this situation, a gut-wrenching decision must be made between two lives. And these decisions are rarely made with perfect information, leaving people to rely on the best estimates of physicians and wrestle with excruciating probabilities.

This must have been even more difficult in the time of Jesus, when medical expertise was much more limited. How should those impossible decisions be made? Who has the knowledge? Who has the right? There is no record of Jesus speaking on this topic. Perhaps Jesus did speak about abortion but his words were simply not recorded and lost to history. Perhaps we can infer he thought the answer was so obvious that it needed no clarification. Or perhaps we can infer each situation was so personal and unique as to be between a person and God, beyond the realm of religious law.

So, we are left to infer how Jesus would have felt about abortion, based on what we know about his life and teachings. If he were standing in the circumstance of a modern-day Christian, how would he behave? Would Jesus protest outside an abortion clinic? Would Jesus vote for immoral leaders only because they promised to outlaw abortion? Would Jesus expect a woman to choose death over childbirth? Would Jesus expect a woman who was raped to bear the child of her rapist?

The words and actions of many Christians suggest they can respond to the questions above with complete confidence in their answers. Many Christians have read the scriptures and reached a conclusion with absolute certainty on the abortion issue. They are completely convinced about the exact moment life begins. And they are completely clear on the circumstances, if any, that justify ending a pregnancy. And they are confident they are right about who gets to make the decision in the face of any ambiguity. Many feel completely certain that ending a pregnancy at any point after conception is the equivalent of murder. Many others feel completely confident that abortion is perfectly acceptable to God. And, unfortunately, all that certainty can breed a lack of grace for those who think differently.

Inferring absolute truth from partial facts is a risky proposition. And if you believe Jesus really was God, it is even more important not to put words in his mouth. There is simply not enough information to be gleaned from the recorded words and actions of Jesus to say with absolutely certainty what his view was on abortion. And that uncertainty creates room for humility, grace, and open-minded thoughtful discussion. Unfortunately, these are sorely lacking in most conversations about abortion today.

11

"*Christians Are So Judgmental*"
Part 1: Holding the Scales

"Religion... encourages and rewards extreme arrogance: nothing so deadly as a righteous man. Likewise, insecure people with a need to belong will tend to choose those features of religions that help them feel good..."[72]

– *Post from Quora.com*

Nearly 90% of U.S. adults 19-29 think Christians are judgmental.[73] This is perhaps the most common complaint against Christians.

But why is this a complaint? Most people would say they want justice. And you cannot have justice without judging between what is just and what is unjust. Many would say that judging is not necessarily a bad thing. Just about every belief system, even those not associated with a formal religion, have a sense of what is right and what is wrong. Society cannot function with complete moral anarchy, without any mechanism for judgment and accountability.

So, why are judgmental Christians such an anathema to the non-Christian world? I suspect most people who complain about judgmental Christians object not to the existence of judgment in general, but that Christians deem themselves worthy of being the ones to judge.

To understand just who is and is not worthy to judge, we start by understanding two aspects of judgment. The classic Lady Justice from Ancient Greece provides a great framework. The Lady Justice metaphor originates from outside the Christian tradition, but provides a great way of thinking about what it means to judge. If you have seen the image, you will recall she is holding scales in one hand and a sword in the other. These two objects each highlight a different aspect of judgment. First are the scales, which speak to determining whether something is right or wrong. Is a given action, thought, motivation, or entity good or evil, right or wrong? Second, she holds a sword, which speaks to the consequence of the judgment. In other words, what punishment or reward should be provided based on evaluation done by the scales?

Different versions of the "Lady Justice" model have been used throughout history, but the principle of the scales and the sword show up time and again. I suspect most people object to judgmental Christians, not because they think there is no place for a scale and a sword in society, but because they do not think Christians are worthy to wield either.

> It turns out Jesus would probably agree. One of Jesus' most famous quotes is this: "'Don't judge, so that you won't be judged.'"[74]

Holding the scales of judgment requires wisdom and broad knowledge. First, you must fully understand the scales you use to measure, or the definition of right and wrong. On the surface, the scale of right and wrong can seem deceptively easy to read. For instance, it is wrong to kill someone. But what if the killing is in self-defense? How can you be sure it was self-defense? What if the person was not threatening to take my life, but only to harm me? Can I kill someone for threatening to harm me? If so, how much harm justifies killing? A severed arm? A broken leg? A bad sprain? Many seemingly obvious questions of right and wrong become a little more opaque as we look to the margins and apply real world situations.

Second, to hold the scales of justice you must also fully understand the thing you are measuring – the actions, words, and motivations of real people. Perhaps we can assume that actions are fairly objective and can be observed and evaluated based on evidence. But motive and intent are a different story. We can never peer into another person's soul and truly understand their motivations, their personal struggles, or the context behind the actions we see or words we hear. Take the example above, where someone kills another person in self-defense. Did the killer really believe they were in danger, or were they just feeling vindictive? Did they feel more in danger because they had been robbed before or because a friend had been murdered? If so, did the murder of their friend by someone else partially justify the killing of a different person who was attacking them on a different day? Reading through the details of real-world court cases would demonstrate we have a hard enough time just determining facts. And gaining perfect clarity on intent is an order of magnitude more complex. This ambiguity makes the scales of justice too heavy to hold without great care and understanding. Judgment without appropriate knowledge is inherently unjust because it relies too heavily on assumption.

Jesus was an advocate for justice. But his definition of what was just was radically different than anything that had come before. He used different scales. As we discussed earlier, being just was not about adhering to the details of thousands of rules. Being just meant following a simple law, "Love God, and love others as yourself." Being just was more than taking the right actions, it also required having the right intent.

This law appears simple, but because it requires right motivations, it is a dramatically more difficult standard against which to measure. Even if we have perfect knowledge of someone's actions, how can we possibly know their intent? Perhaps this is one reason Jesus taught that God alone is qualified to hold the scales of justice: God alone has sufficient knowledge and wisdom to understand and interpret all the facts and the motivations. Jesus did not hesitate to object when he saw someone passing judgment in a seemingly obvious situation, and he challenged people to think more deeply about right and wrong.

On one occasion, Jesus encountered a group of people who apparently were very judgmental.

> "Jesus told this parable to certain people who had convinced themselves that they were righteous and who looked on everyone else with disgust: 'Two people went up to the temple to pray. One was a Pharisee and the other a tax collector. The Pharisee stood and prayed about himself with these words, "God, I thank you that I'm not like everyone else – crooks, evildoers, adulterers – or even like this tax collector. I fast twice a week. I give a tenth of everything I receive."
>
> But the tax collector stood at a distance. He wouldn't even lift his eyes to look toward heaven. Rather, he struck his chest and said, "God, show mercy to me, a sinner." I tell you, this person went down to his home justified rather than the Pharisee. All who lift themselves up will be brought low, and those who make themselves low will be lifted up.'"[75]

The Pharisee's prayer was judgmental – "I thank you that I am not like these other awful people." His conversation with God was really about how he thought he was better than everyone else, bragging about the good works he had done. The tax collector, whose trade involved taking money from his people by force on behalf of an occupying foreign army, acknowledged his failures and prayed for forgiveness with honesty and humility. None of this could be seen from a casual outside observer. Most of the audience listening to Jesus would have condemned the tax collector and lauded the Pharisee. But God saw things much differently.

With this little story, Jesus highlighted that often our judgment is based on limited information and assumptions about how to interpret what we see. Looks can be deceiving, motivations can be opaque, the scales of justice can be difficult to read. No person has perfect knowledge, so no person is worthy to judge. Most people to some degree understand the complexity of discerning right from wrong in every heart and situation, and so they rightly bristle when a Christian tries to hold the scales of judgment.

Jesus understood how difficult it was to read the scales of justice, and with his words and actions, admonished his followers to leave judgment to God.

12

"Christians Are So Judgmental"
Part 2 : Wielding the Sword

"46% of all Christians said that a lack of effort is generally to blame for a person's poverty, compared with 29% of all non-Christians."[76]

— *Washington Post*

"I am so f——g sick of Christians telling people that their mood disorders are their own fault for not worshiping God enough."[77]

— *Post from Reddit.com*

If reading the scales of justice is too perilous for ordinary people, then wielding the sword of justice is an even greater stretch. Few things are more frustrating to non-Christians than when a Christian attempts to say someone's negative circumstances are judgment for their bad choices.

The subject of defining appropriate consequences for bad actions is particularly difficult because most people know they are not perfect. We all have things we are ashamed of doing or thinking. And even if we admit that we have done something wrong, it is quite another thing to agree we should somehow suffer for that wrong decision. Yet, sometimes we still hear Christians say things like, "This person is in a bad situation only because of choices they have made." Some Christian sects may even claim a natural disaster or disease is God's judgment because a specific group of people did something wrong.

The same thing happened in the time of Jesus. In that society, religious leaders drew an even more direct line between what they saw as sin and negative outcomes in people's lives. Yet Jesus typically had a much different perspective on linking negative outcomes to sinful choices.

> Once, upon encountering a blind man, "...the followers of Jesus asked, 'Rabbi, who sinned so that he was born blind, this man or his parents?' Jesus answered, 'Neither he nor his parents. This happened so that God's mighty works might be displayed in him.'"[78]

Jesus refuted the assumption that every bad outcome was the result of a bad choice. He pointed to a bigger plan, zooming out to a cosmic picture that was beyond what we could understand.

Of course, Jesus was not unrealistic about the linkage between bad choices and bad outcomes. Jesus definitely taught that bad decisions would result in bad consequences. During our life on earth, bad decisions generally have bad consequences. Treating ourselves or others poorly often leads to a less fulfilling and healthy life. But, Jesus also taught that our decisions impact us after our earthly life is over. Below is how Jesus described the ultimate consequences of a life of selfishness and unwillingness to help others.

> "[God] will turn to those on the left and say, 'Away with you, you cursed ones, into the eternal fire prepared for the devil and his demons. For I was hungry, and you didn't feed me. I was thirsty, and you didn't give me a drink. I was a stranger, and you didn't invite me into your home. I was naked, and you didn't give me clothing. I was sick and in prison, and you didn't visit me.'
>
> Then they will reply, 'Lord, when did we ever see you hungry or thirsty or a stranger or naked or sick or in prison, and not help you?' And he will answer, 'I tell you the truth, when you refused to help the least of these my brothers and sisters, you were refusing to help me. And they will go away into eternal punishment, but the righteous will go

into eternal life.'"[79]

It is important to note that the evaluation and judgment above was not carried about by a person, by any Christian. The right to judge was reserved for God alone, and it would be carried out after the sum of each person's life had played out. But even so, Jesus taught that God was not eager to mete out punishment. On the contrary, an overarching theme of the teaching of Jesus is that God freely forgives all who ask. Speaking about his legacy, Jesus said,

> "'This message would be proclaimed in the authority of [Jesus' name] to all the nations, beginning in Jerusalem: There is forgiveness of sins for all who repent.'"[80]

Time after time, when he encountered someone who had done something horrible, the first response of Jesus was to forgive, not punish. On one occasion, the religious leaders brought a woman to Jesus who had been caught committing adultery.

> "...Placing her in the center of the group, they said to Jesus, 'Teacher, this woman was caught in the act of committing adultery. In the Law, Moses commanded us to stone women like this. What do you say?' ...Jesus bent down and wrote on the ground with his finger. They continued to question him, so he stood up and replied, 'Whoever hasn't sinned should throw the first stone.' Bending down again, he wrote on the ground. Those who heard

him went away, one by one, beginning with the elders. Finally, only Jesus and the woman were left in the middle of the crowd. Jesus stood up and said to her, 'Woman, where are they? Is there no one to condemn you?' She said, 'No one, sir.' Jesus said, 'Neither do I condemn you. Go, and from now on, don't sin anymore.'"[81]

A self-righteous mob wanted to judge and punish. And, based on the law of that day, punishment would have been completely legal and justified. But Jesus had a different approach. Jesus did not blame and punish and belittle. He understood and extended grace.

One of Jesus' closest followers, who was with Jesus almost continuously for several years, distilled his experience with Jesus this way:

> "God didn't send [Jesus] into the world to judge the world, but that the world might be saved through him."[82]

During one discussion with religious leaders on the subject of judgment, Jesus advised them to study a quote from the old Hebrew teacher Hosea.

> "Go and learn what this means [that Hosea said]: 'I want mercy and not sacrifice. I didn't come to call righteous people, but sinners.'"[83]

Jesus saw his primary mission was not to punish, but to reconcile. When the religious community was defining consequences, Jesus was extending grace. When faced with the choice to punish or embrace, Jesus always embraced. Those who believe Jesus was who he said he was, the embodiment of God on earth, should logically believe that he was the one human most worthy to wield the sword of justice, to punish evil with pain and consequence. Yet he chose not to. Rather than enforce consequences, he died for the greater cause of reconciliation.

13

"*Christians Want To Enforce Their Views on Everyone Else*"
Leading Like a Shepherd

"*...So, whilst I can see why you would do your own thing in your private communities, why do you try to regulate our behavior by condemning the sexual revolution, trying to sneakily limit abortion rights, even complaining because strong women rather than submissive ones are being more widely portrayed in fiction, etc.? Because you are trying to police our life; but we are not forcing you to have abortions and sex before marriage, though. So why don't you just leave us alone?*"[84]

– Post on Reddit.com

Christians believe it is their duty to share God with the world. But this imperative to proselytize is not universal among world religions. Notably Judaism, which shares canon and many beliefs with Christianity, does not evangelize. Perhaps the only religion that places as great of an importance on evangelism is Islam. To people not raised in a Christian or Islamic culture, the Christian desire to share their faith can seem strange or even offensive.

Some of the opposition to Christian evangelism is likely rooted in its historical legacy. The ideal of Christian evangelism is simply to share the same good news that Jesus shared, to help people understand a path to being reconciled with a loving God. Unfortunately, throughout history the reality of evangelism has strayed far from this ideal. The Christian church, Catholic and Protestant alike, has often pursued converts through conquest, war, legislation, and subjugation. The crusades, the Spanish Inquisition, and the subjugation of indigenous people in the Americas and Africa all were to some extent carried out under the banner of Christian evangelism.

Today's Christian churches generally do not attempt to convince people to follow Jesus by using violence. But too often secular society gets the sense that Christians are still bent on subjugation. Christians place immense importance on the distinction between right and wrong, and often speak the loudest when highlighting areas where individuals, or society as a whole, is doing something that is contrary to Christian beliefs. To use religious parlance, Christians often lead with the law rather than leading with grace. So, the Christian imperative of evangelism, although ideally rooted in love, often plays out as a call to compliance.

In the public arena, this often manifests as advocacy for political positions on cultural issues, government policy changes, or even condemnation of individuals or whole groups of people. Aggressively advocating for laws and government policies under the banner of building a "Christian America" can strike fear and stoke anger in the hearts of those of other faiths and atheists alike. The idea of using cultural and political power to force people to live a Christian lifestyle evokes dark comparisons to the times in history the Christian church has been an oppressor, or even to the faith-based Shariah Law that is an oppressive force in many Muslim nations.

The upshot is, instead of feeling that Christians love them, many non-Christians feel Christians are just trying to control them.

Christians may feel these comparisons and concerns are unjustified, and truly believe their motives are rooted in love. But nonetheless, this deep distaste for Christian control is very real, and causes many people to not explore the person of Jesus Christ. This is ironic and unfortunate, because during his lifetime Jesus spoke very little about rules and made no effort to control people. On the contrary, he had little tolerance for religious leaders who used rules to control people or reinforce their own superiority.

> "Jesus said, 'How terrible for you legal experts too! You load people down with impossible burdens and you refuse to lift a single finger to help them.'"[85]

While Jesus was not focused on imposing rules on people, or layering new laws on top of old ones, he was not just a passive observer to the world around him. Jesus was very much an agent of change, and he had a massive influence on those around him. But the model of influence Jesus used is much different from what we see so many Christians model today. The first interaction Jesus had with Peter provides a great example of how Jesus influenced people.

> Peter was a fisherman by trade and had a very unsuccessful day on the water. "Jesus.... said to [him], 'Row out farther, into the deep water, and drop your nets for a catch.' Simon replied, 'Master, we've worked hard all night and caught nothing. But because you say so, I'll drop the nets.' So, they dropped the nets and their catch was so huge that their nets were splitting. When Simon Peter saw the catch, he fell at Jesus' knees and said, 'Leave me, Lord, for I'm a sinner!' ...Peter and those with him were overcome with amazement because of the number of fish they caught... Jesus said to Simon, 'Don't be afraid. From now on, you will be fishing for people.' As soon as they brought the boats to the shore, they left everything and followed Jesus."[86]

First, Jesus took the time to understand Peter's situation. He got aboard Peter's boat. He would have seen there was no fish and that Peter and the crew were tired. Next, he helped meet the material need he saw by providing a great catch of fish. At this point, everyone was amazed, both by the miracle of such a large catch, and likely also by the fact that someone with such power would take a personal interest in helping an ordinary fisherman.

Then, faced by the evidence of a very real God, Peter immediately acknowledged his own failures. "Lord… I am a sinner." Notice there is no record of Jesus pointing out any sin or wrongdoing in Peter's life. Peter, like the rest of us, probably was already well aware of his own failures and shortcomings. Rather than chronicle for Peter everything he was doing that was bad, Jesus just provided an example of what was good. And the impact on Peter was far more powerful.

At this point, Jesus had everyone's attention. Everyone was amazed by the miracle and would have been hanging on his every word. But he used this spotlight in a way that is very rare in our society today. Jesus did not try to use this moment to expand his power or control. He did not lean into Peter's admission of guilt and give him a lengthy list of things to do and rules to follow. Jesus did not try to influence from the outside by exerting control over Peter.

Instead, Jesus influenced from the inside out by focusing on the motivation within Peter's heart. "From now on, you'll be fishing for people." Jesus called Peter to a life that served others, to putting other people first. He invited Peter to make the "love your neighbor as yourself" command the guiding force in his life, because Jesus knew that our words and actions flow out of the motivations of our hearts.

A final insight into how Jesus influenced is provided right at the end of this account, when the passage says, "they… followed Jesus." This does not suggest Jesus driving people like cattle with noise and prodding. It does not suggest chasing people with fear like a predator chasing prey.

Jesus wanted to lead like a shepherd. He wanted to influence people to follow him willingly, because they have a relationship with him. On another occasion he said, "'I am the good shepherd. I know my own sheep and they know me.'"[87]

Jesus was absolutely an agent of change, who wanted to have a positive influence on people's lives. But he did not want to control people from the outside in by imposing rules on people who did not agree with him. Rather he wanted to inspire people to follow him by getting to know them, meeting their needs, and providing a living example of a better way. Jesus did not lead by controlling, he led by example. And people followed of their own free will.

14

"*Christians Expect Me To Believe Everything in The Bible*"
God or Book About God?

"I don't care what it says in your holy book. I don't care what they told you in your church... etc. No, I don't have to respect your beliefs. Most of all I don't care what you think your imaginary god(s) told you."[88]

– *Post on Quora.com*

Even when viewed through a secular lens, the Christian Bible is a remarkable work, filled with wisdom, poetry, history, and revelation. But, Christians believe the Bible is far more than just a historical text. Most Christians believe the Bible to be inspired by God. As such it becomes the ultimate source of truth.

Based on this belief, Christians can often find a passage of scripture to apply to just about any situation, to justify each of their opinions. A Christian children's song famously says, "Jesus loves me, because the Bible tells me so." And for many, that is evidence enough. Christians fiercely defend their view that the Bible is infallible. It can sometimes be difficult to determine whether Christianity is faith in Christ or faith in the Bible. The distinction is subtle, but critical.

Other religions have sacred texts that offer a view of how humankind relates to the divine and provides instructions for how followers should conduct their lives. Islam, Judaism, Buddhism, and others all have a canon that carries the weight of divine credibility for its adherents. The Christian Bible serves this same function. But the Christian faith is not based on the Bible, it is based on the person of Jesus Christ. This distinction, while subtle, can have a profound impact on how Christians communicate with those outside the faith.

To a Christian who is discussing an ethical issue or even the nature of God with a non-Christian, it is only natural to point to passages in the Bible to justify a given position. And of course, the Bible is an excellent source. But, while the Christian views the book as the ultimate authority, the person they are speaking with views it as just another data point to be proven or disproven. And because Christians often speak of the Bible as a single perfect monolithic work, if someone does not believe part of it, they can dismiss the entire book as untrue.

Few non-Christians people have the time, interest, or ability to validate the accuracy of the entire 783,000 words in the Bible. But it is quite easy to latch on to one or two things that seem inaccurate and use that to justify dismissing the entire compilation. This is the "dinosaur problem," where the thought process goes like this:

1. Christians say the entire Bible is the infallible word of God.
2. A literal interpretation of the Bible says dinosaurs did not exist.
3. I have seen actual dinosaur bones in a museum.
4. So, the whole Bible must be wrong, including whatever it says about Jesus.

In this way, the more a Christian tries to insist every literal word of the entire Bible is absolute truth, the more it can be difficult to use scripture to tell the world about Jesus.

But what did Jesus say about scripture? To understand what Jesus thought about the scriptures that comprise the Bible, and how he applied them, we need to first understand what this book is, and how it came to be.

The Bible is a compilation of texts, including works from as many as forty authors written over a span of about two thousand years. Most Christians believe the Bible to have been inspired by God. This need not be an overly mystical or magical assumption. Inspired by God does not necessarily mean every actual word was handed down from heaven on a scroll. Rather it means that God shared insight and wisdom with a series of people over many years, and these people wrote down what they felt God spoke to them.

The oldest and largest portion of the Bible, the section Christians refer to as the "Old Testament," is essentially the same Hebrew canon that was compiled over the two thousand years or so leading up to the birth of Christ. Adherents to the Jewish faith may refer to these books collectively as the Tanakh. The Tanakh includes twenty-four books, grouped into three sections. The first five books are called the Torah or Pentateuch, and include the creation account, early history of the Jewish people, and the law of Moses. The Nevi'im, or books of the prophets, detail the history of the Jewish people through hundreds of years of peace, war, exile, and redemption. These books are predominantly written through the lens of the prophets, or people Jews and Christians believe were sent by God to help reconcile his people to himself. The final group of books is the Ketuvim, or "Writings," which include books of poetry, wisdom, and history. Psalms and Proverbs are likely the most familiar books of the Ketuvim.[89][90]

Collectively, these works that comprise the Old Testament are almost universally recognized by Christian sects as being part of the Bible. However, the remainder of the Bible, collectively called the New Testament, is often given more weight and treated as more important by some Christians, especially those in the Catholic tradition. The New Testament, which was written after the birth of Jesus of Nazareth, focuses on the life of Jesus, the teachings of his followers immediately after his death, and events that took place in the early years of the movement that would eventually be called Christianity.

The New Testament contains four groups of books. First is a compilation of first-person accounts of the life of Jesus. These are often referred to as the Gospels, which is derived from a Greek word meaning "Good News." These four books offer parallel descriptions of the life of Jesus, from four different people who were with him throughout his ministry. Next is a book named "Acts" or "Acts of the Apostles" which chronicles the early history of the Christian church. After that we find the Epistles, which is derived from a Greek word roughly translated as "send news." Epistles were letters written by early Christian leaders, some of whom had known Jesus personally, to communities of Jesus followers all around the Mediterranean. The final book of the New Testament is Revelation, which is full of symbolism and is believed to contain prophecies about future events. [91]

In the years following the death of Jesus, a great many works were written about Jesus and the God he spoke about. And, the debate over which of these writings to include in the Christian Bible lasted for decades. Ultimately, a gathering of Christian leaders in A.D. 381 compiled a collection closely resembling today's Bible based on a specific set of criteria. For a text to be included, it needed to be:

- Written by one of Jesus' disciples, someone who was a witness to Jesus' ministry, such as Peter, or someone who interviewed witnesses, such as Luke.

- Written in the first century A.D., meaning that books written long after the events of Jesus' life and the first decades of the church weren't included.

- Consistent with other portions of the Bible known to be

valid, meaning the book couldn't contradict a trusted element of Scripture.[92]

Although the debate was mostly resolved by A.D. 400, a few differences still remain. The Catholic Church uses a Bible slightly different from the Protestant denominations, with seven additional books in the Bible, as well as some additions to the books of Daniel and Esther.[93]

In addition, it is important to note that the Bible was not originally written in English. The subset of the Bible referred to as the "Old Testament" was originally written in Hebrew, although much of it was passed down orally for many generations before the first manuscripts were created. The subset of books written after the birth of Jesus, or the "New Testament" was originally written in Greek, although Jesus and his closest disciples predominantly spoke Aramaic. Every word we read in an English Bible has been translated based on an interpretation of the original text from another language. Of course, there is subjectivity and potential bias in the process of compiling and translating texts written hundreds of years earlier, in cultural contexts much different than our own. These varying interpretations have resulted in around eight hundred different translations in English alone, not to mention all the other world languages.

While the specific wording of each translation varies, in general the underlying content is consistent. A good example is Amos 4:6. In the King James Version of the Bible, one of the oldest and most widely used translations, the verse reads as follows:

> "And I also have given you cleanness of teeth in all your cities, and want of bread in all your places: yet have ye not returned unto me, saith the Lord."

However, in the New Living Translation, a relatively newer translation, the verse reads somewhat differently.

> "I brought hunger to every city and famine to every town. But still you would not return to me," says the Lord."

The King James Version almost directly translated the Hebrew words for "clean teeth", which in today's culture speaks of dental health. But when Amos, the original author, was alive, "clean teeth" was an idiom for being hungry and having no food. The newer translation bypassed the idiom, since it is no longer widely used, and instead used the underlying meaning that today's readers would understand.[94]

Some Christians deny these elements of subjectivity in the Bible, and claim that every phrase includes the literal words of God. Some non-Christians point to the variations in language as proof that the compilation cannot possibly be divinely inspired. But both of these views potentially miss the entire point of the Bible by viewing it as a collection of facts and explicit statements. A better way to view the Bible is as a vast collection of truths, a story about the relationship between God and humankind. For instance, great arguments have been had over whether or not it is a fact that God created the earth in seven twenty-four hour days. But, to debate the validity of the interpretation of that fact is to miss the broader and much more important truth that there is a God who created the earth and longs to interact with the creatures that live on it.

So, what did Jesus say about scripture and how it should be used? How did he incorporate sacred texts in his daily life and ministry?

First, Jesus validated that scripture should exist and play a prominent role in our lives and our understanding of God. He repeatedly affirmed the truth and relevance of the Tanakh, or Old Testament. Jesus was Jewish, raised in a culture that was familiar with, and even defined by, this compilation of writings. Jesus taught that his life and words were consistent with this older canon, a continuation of the thread of revealed truth that began with the first words written thousands of years previously.

> On one occasion, Jesus said, "'Don't think that I have come to abolish the Torah or the Prophets. I have come not to abolish but to complete…'"[95]

Understanding what Jesus might have said about the New Testament is a little more difficult, because those books were not written at the time of his earthly ministry. The books that comprise the New Testament were mostly written in the first century AD, in the decades immediately following the ministry of Jesus.[96]

But, Jesus did make it clear that his words and teachings carried the same weight as the existing canon. He said on several occasions that he was speaking words given to him by God.

"'I don't speak on my own, but the Father who sent me commanded me regarding what I should speak and say. I know that his commandment is eternal life. Therefore, whatever I say is just as the Father has said to me.'"[97]

Many Christians extend the weight of passages like this to the Epistles and the other books of the New Testament. They believe that when Jesus spoke about scripture in his teaching, he used the term broadly to refer to additional works that would be written later. But Jesus made no direct reference to future books that would be written by others and carry the same canonical weight as his own words.

Jesus intended his words and actions to be documented, remembered, and shared.

> Jesus said, "'Everybody who hears these words of mine and puts them into practice is like a wise builder who built a house on bedrock.'"[98]
>
> And, "'Heaven and earth will pass away, but my words will certainly not pass away.'"[99]
>
> "'Go therefore and make disciples of all the nations [help the people to learn of Me, believe in Me, and obey My words]... teaching them to observe everything that I have commanded you...'"[100]

So, it seems clear that Jesus supported the importance of having scripture, documentation that taught about God's relationship with humankind. And he made it clear his teaching should be a part of that canon. To Jesus, scripture was an essential and invaluable tool for people to learn about God. In this way, modern Christians who greatly value the Bible are aligned with Christ. But, beyond just affirming the value of scripture, the way Jesus communicated it and applied it are much different than what we often see in our society today.

Jesus did not just pick a few passages and share them out of context. Jesus demonstrated a deep understanding of the scriptures, frequently weaving passages naturally into conversation. There are 180 recorded occasions where Jesus referenced the Old Testament, either by directly quoting passages or referring to specific parts.[101]

And Jesus went beyond simply quoting the text word for word, he also understood the context in which scriptures were written. He demonstrated that understanding the context of the scripture was key to understanding what the words were intended to communicate. For instance, consider this exchange on the subject of divorce.

> "[Jesus] said, 'This explains why a man leaves his father and mother and is joined to his wife, and the two are united into one. Since they are no longer two but one, let no one split apart what God has joined together.'

> "'Then why did Moses say in the law that a man could give his wife a written notice of divorce and send her away?' they asked.
>
> "Jesus replied, 'Moses permitted divorce only as a concession to your hard hearts, but it was not what God had originally intended.'"[102]

In that culture, a man divorcing his wife could doom her to a life of poverty and make her a social pariah. Yet, it was permitted under the law. Jesus provided context about why the law was written a certain way and pointed to a broader truth: that marriage is designed to be two souls united equally as one for a lifetime.

When discussing scripture, Jesus generally focused on broad truths rather than esoteric facts. People would frequently bring him a narrow, literal passage, and he would redirect them to a broader truth. This passage about relating to enemies we discussed earlier is a great example.

> "You have heard the law that says the punishment must match the injury: 'An eye for an eye, and a tooth for a tooth.' But I say, do not resist an evil person! If someone slaps you on the right cheek, offer the other cheek also.
>
> "You have heard the law that says, 'Love your neighbor'… But I say, love your enemies! Pray for those who persecute you! In that way, you will be acting as true children of your Father in heaven.'"[103]

Jesus did not focus on the detailed interpretation of the specific punishment that should be meted out according to the law. Rather, he reframed the discussion to a broader truth that love and forgiveness was a higher way than punishment.

Jesus also demonstrated that scriptures are not just something to be read and blindly repeated. Jesus actively studied scriptures, and frequently engaged in debate and discussion about how to interpret the words. There were many instances where people asked Jesus about the meaning of a passage, and he engaged in a conversation about it. Even at an early age Jesus was actively debating the meaning of scripture.

> "When he was twelve years old, they went up to Jerusalem according to their custom. After the festival was over, they were returning home, but the boy Jesus stayed behind in Jerusalem. His parents didn't know. After three days they found him in the temple. He was sitting among the teachers, listening to them and asking them questions. Everyone who heard him was amazed by his understanding and his answers."[104]

Jesus invited and encouraged questions about scripture. Truth does not need to shy away from scrutiny. Truth only gets stronger the more it is questioned.

Jesus also clearly pointed out how scripture could be misused and be destructive. Matthew records a story Jesus told about how he was tempted by Satan. And in the story Jesus told, Satan quoted scripture out of context in an attempt to cause Jesus to harm himself.

> "Then the devil took him to the holy city, Jerusalem, to the highest point of the Temple, and said, 'If you are the Son of God, jump off! For the Scriptures say, He will order his angels to protect you. And they will hold you up with their hands so you won't even hurt your foot on a stone.'"[105]

In this example, someone with evil intent was quoting scripture as a means of manipulating Jesus into marking a bad choice. So many through history have done this, using isolated scripture out of context to cause pain in the world. It was the same in the time of Jesus. But he offered this brief story as a warning about the danger of taking scripture out of context.

Lastly, Jesus did not say believing every word of the Christian Bible to be the literal fallible word of God is a requirement for spiritual salvation. Believing in Jesus is the sole requirement for salvation.

> "God so loved the world that he gave his only Son, so that everyone who believes in him won't perish but will have eternal life."[106]

Some Christians will say that Jesus is the word of God, so believing in him is synonymous with believing the Bible. John, one of the closest disciples of Jesus, wrote this about him.

> "In the beginning was the Word, and the Word was with God, and the Word was God. He was with God in the beginning. All things came to be through him, and without him nothing made had being. In him was life, and the life was the light of mankind. The light shines in the darkness, and the darkness has not suppressed it."[107]

But "Word" in this scripture refers to something far more powerful than a written text. The original Greek word John used is "Logos," which refers to the actual embodiment of the revelation of God. "In the Greek worldview, the Logos was thought of as a bridge between the transcendent God and the material universe." [108] John was not saying scriptures were the embodiment of Jesus, he was saying Jesus was the embodiment of God.

There are many instances of Jesus calling someone to follow him. Yet, in none of these cases did he require the person read the scripture, much less attest to the literal infallibility of the translation. We see a fitting example of this in the final moments before Jesus' death, as he spoke with a criminal that was being executed beside him.

> "They also led two other criminals to be executed with Jesus. When they arrived at the place called The Skull, they crucified him, along with the criminals, one on his right and the other on his left.
>
> "One of the criminals hanging next to Jesus insulted him: 'Aren't you the Christ? Save yourself and us!'

"Responding, the other criminal spoke harshly to him, 'Don't you fear God, seeing that you've also been sentenced to die? We are rightly condemned, for we are receiving the appropriate sentence for what we did. But this man has done nothing wrong.' Then he said, 'Jesus, remember me when you come into your kingdom.'

"Jesus replied, 'I assure you that today you will be with me in paradise.'"[109]

This criminal was saved, promised a place in a pleasant afterlife, simply because he professed faith in Jesus and recognized him as the embodiment of God. There was no requirement that he attest to the infallibility of scripture.

In fact, the Christian community enjoyed rapid growth before the New Testament scriptures were ever written. A few days after Jesus left the earth, there was a great stir in Jerusalem as his followers began to share their account of what had happened. Thousands of people gathered around Jesus' closest followers to listen, to mock, or just to watch curiously. Peter stood and spoke for several minutes, using passages from the Tanakh mixed with his own personal experience with Jesus. Over three thousand people became followers of Jesus after hearing what Peter said.[110]

And the growth did not stop there. The Christian church grew to over two million people by AD 250, about two hundred years after the crucifixion of Jesus. And, while the various writings that make up the New Testament were written in the decades immediately following the death of Jesus, the Bible in its current form was not compiled until around 400 AD. [111] [112]

For those who do not believe in God, or believe the Bible is inspired by God, it is still an incredibly valuable resource for learning about the transformative historical figure known as Jesus of Nazareth. It is by far the most comprehensive record we have of the life and teachings of Jesus Christ, and the early years of the Christian movement that bears his name. It contains letters written by people that knew Jesus personally. As such, it is the absolute best resource for learning about Jesus, and an indispensable guidebook for following him.

For those who do believe in the God described in the Bible, those writings are the greatest compilation of insight and knowledge into who God is, and how God relates to mankind. It was compiled by people who had remarkable encounters with God and deep relationships with God. It includes historical accounts, descriptions of miracles, compelling parables, poetry, and great wisdom. It has been researched and analyzed and debated over centuries. It still has the same powerful impact in a time of computers and rocket ships as it did in a time of crude tools and dusty streets. There is compelling evidence the book was divinely inspired.

But, while the Bible is our best guidebook to God, the book is not God. The foundation of the Christian faith is Christ, not a book. The distinction is critical. Words can be taken out of context, misinterpreted, misused, misunderstood. But a relationship with God is always transformative for good. The scriptures have been used to cause a lot of pain and destruction through the centuries. But the person of Jesus brought nothing but good. Knowing scripture is only important because it is a means to the greater end of knowing God.

Jesus was continually questioned by religious leaders who were experts in the minutia of scripture. But Jesus suggested their knowledge was incomplete, not just because they did not fully understand the scriptures, but also because they did not know the God the scriptures were meant to reveal.

> Jesus said to the religious leaders, "'Your mistake is that you don't know the Scriptures, and you don't know the power of God.'"[113]

They missed the forest because they were so focused on the trees. In our modern day, it might be like spending so much time debating whether creation occurred in exactly seven twenty-four-hour days, that we miss the broader truth that there is a God who is very real and very intentionally created this world for us.

There may be nothing more tragic than a person who never gets to know the God of the scriptures because they do not believe some esoteric fact in the scriptures.

> Was the book of Job a historical account or a parable?
> Did every species on the earth really fit into an ark?
> When were dinosaurs on the earth?

Trying to find the answers to these questions in the Bible

requires reviewing ancient texts that document verbal records passed from person to person over hundreds of generations. There is nothing wrong with trying to answer those questions. But answers to these questions should never be roadblocks to answering much more important questions that are core to the Christian faith.

>Does God love me and want a relationship with me?
>Did God come to earth in the person of Jesus?
>Do I have eternal hope?

Perhaps the most compelling insight about how Jesus viewed scriptures was distilled when he said these words:

>"'And you will know the truth, and the truth will set you free.'"[114]

Jesus focused on the incredible impact of truth revealed. Jesus did not need to spend a lot of time debating whether or not specific esoteric facts from the scriptures were accurate. He did not get into deep arguments about why the scriptures were or were not real. Jesus believed the words of God, the truth of God, had power to move hearts and minds.

The transformative impact of scripture is the most compelling argument for its veracity. Said another way, we can spend hours piling up evidence from archaeology and ancient history to prove the Bible is true. And we can engage in impassioned arguments to convince people the Bible is the word of God. But as compelling as those arguments may be, they will never be as powerful as the conviction that comes when someone reads a passage and feels God draw near.

Jesus had a deep understanding of scripture and did not simply quote single passages out of context. He focused on broad truths rather than engage in debates over minutiae. He did not use scripture to control people, but to point people to God. And he believed the truth of God has a power to impact people for good.

This boldness and confidence, grounded in great understanding and without a whisper of defensiveness, characterized how Jesus communicated the scriptures.

> No wonder Matthew said, "...the crowds were amazed at his teaching, for he taught with real authority – quite unlike their teachers of religious law."[115]

The difference in how Jesus used the scriptures was remarkable then and would be even more so today.

15

"*Christians Do Not Believe in Science*"
The Faith of an Open Mind

"As an atheist, my criticism of religion is not really what it thinks about reality, but rather how it thinks about reality. In point of fact, the religious don't think about reality at all. They think about their beliefs. Eyes clamped shut.

Science, on the other hand, doesn't give a damn what anybody believes. Science wants to know what you saw, whether everybody who looked saw the same thing, and what mechanisms best explain what everybody saw. Eyes wide open.

> *I don't mind religion. I just don't understand why people with their eyes clamped shut are so excited to tell the rest of us what they see."*[116]
>
> – Post on Quora.com

Many people, including some Christians, see a natural conflict between faith and science. They point to a series of apparently irreconcilable areas where Christians and the secular scientific community disagree as to objective facts. For instance:

- The age of the universe: Modern scientific methods estimate the earth is around 4.5 billion years old, while a literal interpretation of the Bible suggests the earth is only six to ten thousand years old.

- The origin of life: Christians believe living things were intentionally created by God, while secular science believes living things are the outcome of random mutation.

- The existence of miracles: Christians believe God sometimes intervenes in the natural world in ways that cannot be explained by science as it stands today. For instance: miraculous healing, visions of the future, inner peace in the midst of trauma.

Science is a discipline built on observation and testing as a means of discovery. The Oxford Dictionary defines the scientific method as:

> "A method of procedure that has characterized natural science since the 17th century, consisting in systematic observation, measurement, and experiment, and the formulation, testing, and modification of hypotheses."[117] Criticism is the backbone of the scientific method.

So, when Christians hold a belief to be beyond the reach of science, they are essentially resisting any challenge to that belief. They are saying that scientific principles of observation and study do not apply. Christians may feel strong when they do this and celebrate resisting the tide of scientific questions by responding with a simple declaration of faith: "I just believe it is true." But to many, a Christian who resists the probe of tough questions with a simple declaration of belief communicates that their faith is weak. How strong is a truth that cannot stand up to scrutiny? Playing the "because the Bible said so" or "it's just what I believe" card may affirm a Christian's own internal sense of faith, but it does little to build faith in others. Science seeks to discover unrevealed truth by challenging everything with rigorous questions, and so is often at odds with modern Christians. But would that scientific approach be at odds with Jesus?

Jesus certainly emphasized the importance and power of faith.

> "'What do you mean, if...?' Jesus asked. 'Anything is possible if a person believes.'"[118]

Jesus taught that faith in God was a key to making the connection between the earthly and the eternal. Simply put, God gets more directly involved in our lives when we believe he exists.

> "Jesus responded, 'Didn't I tell you that you would see God's glory if you believe?'"[119]

Similarly, Jesus taught that God was less likely to intervene on our behalf if we do not believe.

> Referring to one town in particular that Jesus frequented, Matthew wrote, "And so [Jesus] did only a few miracles there because of their unbelief."[120]

Yet, while Jesus placed immense importance on faith, he was also willing to provide proof when people had genuine honest questions. John the Baptist, a teacher whose ministry began before Jesus became known, sent people to honestly inquire about the claims of Jesus. Luke records it this way:

> "...John the Baptist... sent [two of his followers] to [Jesus] to ask him, 'Are you the Messiah we've been expecting, or should we keep looking for someone else?'"

> Jesus did not berate John's messengers for asking questions or seeking proof. Instead, he told John's disciples, "'Go back to John and tell him what you have seen and heard – the blind see, the lame walk, those with leprosy are cured, the deaf hear, the dead are raised to life, and the Good News is being preached to the poor.'"[121]

Jesus did not say, "I am the Messiah; just believe me." He did things to provide evidence he was divine and did not hesitate to communicate these proof points to John the Baptist.

On another occasion, Jesus invited the local authorities to validate one of his miracles of healing.

> "...Jesus met a man with an advanced case of leprosy. When the man saw Jesus, he bowed with his face to the ground, begging to be healed. 'Lord,' he said, 'if you are willing, you can heal me and make me clean.'
>
> "Jesus reached out and touched him. 'I am willing,' he said. 'Be healed!' And instantly the leprosy disappeared. Then Jesus instructed him not to tell anyone what had happened. He said, 'Go to the priest and let him examine you. Take along the offering required in the law of Moses for those who have been healed of leprosy. This will be a public testimony that you have been cleansed.'"[122]

In those days, there were documented procedures for proving whether someone had leprosy. Jesus did not say, "Just believe in your healing and ignore the experts." Rather, he told the man he healed to get thoroughly examined, to seek public confirmation of his healing. As was often the case with the works of Jesus, faith and objective confirmation went hand in hand.

Jesus used scientific principles to illustrate principles of faith.[123]

This suggests that Jesus was knowledgeable about science, but also that he saw a symbiosis between the two, with each reinforcing the other. For instance, on one occasion he used the process of plant germination to illustrate how different people receive truth.

> "When a great crowd was gathering… Jesus… spoke to them in a parable: 'A farmer went out to scatter his seed. As he was scattering it, some fell on the path where it was crushed, and the birds in the sky came and ate it. Other seed fell on rock. As it grew, it dried up because it had no moisture. Other seed fell among thorny plants. The thorns grew with the plants and choked them. Still other seed landed on good soil. When it grew, it produced one hundred times more grain than was scattered.' As he said this, he called out, 'Everyone who has ears should pay attention.' He said, 'You have been given the mysteries of God's kingdom, but these mysteries come to everyone else in parables…'"[124]

Truths about God and how he relates to mankind are embedded in the natural world, and that world is illuminated by science. Prominent scientists have echoed the same insight, that science can inform faith and vice versa.

> Former NASA Director Werner von Braun wrote: "The vast mysteries of the universe should only confirm our belief in the certainty of its Creator. I find it as difficult to understand a scientist who

does not acknowledge the presence of a superior rationality behind... the universe, as it is to comprehend a theologian who would deny the advances of science."

German astronomer Johann Kepler, one of the greatest scientists of the seventeenth century, described scientific discovery simply as, "Thinking God's thoughts after Him."[125]

An early follower of Jesus, Paul of Tarsus, summarized the relationship between faith and natural science like this:

> "Ever since the creation of the world, God's invisible qualities – God's eternal power and divine nature – have been clearly seen, because they are understood through the things God has made. So, humans are without excuse."[126]

Science is a way to understand God and, similarly, faith in God opens up whole new avenues of scientific discovery.

Jesus also taught there was great danger in becoming closed-minded to new information. He even quoted an old passage from Isaiah that spoke of close-mindedness as a form of God's punishment.

> "Jesus said, 'What Isaiah prophesied has become completely true for them: You will hear, to be sure, but never understand; and you will certainly see

but never recognize what you are seeing. For this people's senses have become calloused, and they've become hard of hearing, and they've shut their eyes so that they won't see with their eyes or hear with their ears or understand with their minds, and change their hearts and lives that I may heal them. Happy are your eyes because they see. Happy are your ears because they hear.'"[127]

The people described here were cut off from expanding their knowledge because they no longer listened and took in new information. Their minds were closed.

Jesus also did not hesitate to challenge and reprimand learned people who withheld knowledge from the broader population. When speaking to a group of the most learned people in Hebrew society, Jesus said,

> "'How terrible for you legal experts! You snatched away the key of knowledge. You didn't enter yourselves, and you stood in the way of those who were entering.'"[128]

These were people who refused to learn, and blocked other people from learning. Jesus said this opposition to sharing of knowledge was terrible.

Jesus also acknowledged there are things we simply are not able to understand.

> "Jesus replied, 'You don't understand what I'm doing now, but you will understand later.'"[129]

There is a passage in the Hebrew wisdom writings that says this:

> "It is God's privilege to conceal things and the king's privilege to discover them. No one can comprehend the height of heaven, the depth of the earth…"[130]

There is a fundamental humility to faith in God because the existence of God suggests there is something beyond our understanding. This truth ought to make all Christians humble both on matters of faith and science. There is always more to understand, so there are always questions to be asked. And there will be times when those questions just do not have answers. Unanswered questions are not evil or dangerous; they are opportunities for truth to be discovered, for God to be revealed.

The prevailing cultural perspective states there is a conflict between science and faith. But that opinion shows either a lack of understanding of true faith or a lack of understanding of true science. Faith is belief in a higher truth. Science is seeking truth by asking questions and trying to find answers. Both faith and science acknowledge there are some things that are simply too big and complex to understand. There may be no greater symbiosis than that between true faith and true science. Scientists believe there are bigger things, higher truths we cannot understand but are worth seeking. People of faith believe the same.[131] In fact, some of the greatest scientists of all time were men of deep faith: Isaac Newton, Michael Faraday, Werner Heisenberg, and dozens more. [132]

> The Hebrew prophet Isaiah, a great man of faith, mourned the tragedy of close-mindedness when he said, "For this people's senses have become calloused, and they've become hard of hearing, and they've shut their eyes so that they won't see with their eyes or hear with their ears or understand with their minds..." Jesus later quoted this passage to express his sadness over the close-mindedness he saw in his time.
>
> Thousands of years later, scientist and futurist Isaac Asimov said, "Your assumptions are your windows on the world. Scrub them off every once in a while, or the light won't come in."[133]

The real conflict is not between science and faith, but between close mindedness and open mindedness. Or, to use the words of Isaiah, between "shutting your eyes so you cannot see" and constantly looking for truth and understanding. It is not fair to criticize Christians for having a different point of view about the timeline of creation, the moment life begins, or other areas of natural history. Many scientists disagree with each other and have competing theories. But it might be fair to take issue with Christians who will not engage in open-minded, objective debate on these topics, or who refuse to martial facts outside of scripture to support their point of view.

When faced with a scientific discovery that appears to conflict with a religious belief or passage of scripture, many Christians take pride in confirming their belief and quickly dismissing any competing view. There is often a sense that refusing to question one's own belief is a sign of strong faith. But, it could be a sign of weakness. The truth has nothing to fear from being questioned.

Ironically, refusing to engage with science or doing the work to understand how scientific discoveries challenge and expand beliefs can make it more difficult for Christians to have a positive impact on the world. For example, many Christians oppose abortion based on scripture from the Old Testament. To a non-Christian, this piece of evidence carries zero weight and feels like religious oppression. But, if Christians study the early development of the fetus in the womb and make the case that the fetus at some point has brain function, can feel pain, even feel emotion, they may find that evidence is much more effective at changing minds than simply quoting scripture. Or, if Christians want to prove the existence of an eternal, ageless God to a skeptical world, they might find a great deal of evidence in the theories that hypothesize a universe where time is just another dimension, or a single dramatic moment when all of creation was set into motion by an unknown force (the "Big Bang").

Jesus did not shy away from weaving together science and faith, or from engaging in difficult discussions. And if the Christian scriptures are true, then God reveals himself in creation, in the natural world. So, relying solely on scriptures and not engaging in scientific discovery discards one of the primary ways God speaks to humankind. Paul's words above are worth repeating:

> "For ever since the world was created, people have seen the earth and sky. Through everything God made, they can clearly see his invisible qualities – his eternal power and divine nature. So, they have no excuse for not knowing God."[134]

This suggests the natural world is a kind of third testament to God. And the testament of nature is universally accessible, even for people who dismiss the Bible as just another book, or for whom the Bible is not available. If God embeds truth in all of creation, imagine the revelation possible if it was studied with the same vigor as the scriptures. That is essentially what science aims to do. And if we take cues from the words of Jesus, that is also how faith grows.

16

"*Christians Feel Like They Are Under Attack*"
So What?

"*In a poll by the anti-defamation league at the end of last year, 64 percent of Americans say religion in America is under attack... Eighty percent of evangelicals agree that religion in this country, in particular, Christianity, is under attack.*" [135]

– Tony Perkins, President, Family Research Council

"73% of white evangelical Republicans believe 'immigrants are invading our country and replacing our cultural and ethnic background.'" [136]

> "Things that are unchristian cannot exist in their world, even though their world affects others. So, when they see things like gay marriage becoming legalized, they claim they are under attack. When they see that sex education is being taught in schools and it's not abstinence only, they feel that they are under attack. When they see that society is accepting premarital sex as okay, they feel they are under attack. When they see increasing amounts of hostility towards creationism, they feel they are under attack. Essentially, if they don't get their way, they are under attack. They're not actually under attack. I'm not under attack. Christianity isn't under attack. It's just not the norm anymore..." [137]
>
> – Post on Quora.com

Many Christians demonstrate a sense of desperation, even fear, as it relates to changing culture. This sense of being under attack has created a kind of siege mentality within parts of the Christian community. The earth is shifting under their feet, and it is scary. The winds of culture are blowing in their face instead of pushing them along from behind. Their beliefs are no longer mainstream. Things they took as obviously true are now being challenged. They worry about what will happen to future generations if this rate of change continues. Christians often come across as ill at ease, unsettled, afraid. They just want to go back to the way things were, when things were simpler, easier.

It is common to hear Christians say, "Christianity is under attack."

Of course, a statement like this begs the question, "Attacked by whom?" In a diverse society, there is almost always some group who is attacking another, so there are certainly people or groups who hate Christians and aggressively attempt to minimize them. Christians most often cite the government or the media as the source of attack.

Yet, it is difficult to find evidence of intentional attack coming from the major government institutions in the U.S., as religious liberties have been repeatedly affirmed by courts at all levels.[138] Defining and defending religious liberty has been a key theme in U.S. politics since before the U.S. technically existed, with many of the original European settlers seeking religious freedom in the new world.[139]

More likely, Christians would cite the media, the entertainment industry, or culture in general as the entity attacking Christians. And there are many examples of individuals aggressively criticizing Christians, and of Christians being portrayed negatively in books, television, and movies. But the media and the entertainment industry are comprised of thousands of separate organizations and individuals. There is no central cabal that controls all media. And if there were, they would probably be far more focused on finding ways to make money than on orchestrating coordinated attacks on Christianity.

Yet, even if there is not a massive, intentional, coordinated campaign against Christianity, there are clearly areas where culture has shifted dramatically in ways that make many Christians uncomfortable. Rather than being the result of a centralized, coordinated attack, the change is more likely the natural culmination of gradual change in millions of individual hearts. But regardless, the traditional values of the Christian church do not hold the sway they once did in our culture.

Comparing the culture and laws in the U.S. today versus when today's seniors were children reveals a stark contrast. Most people today do not go to church. Businesses no longer routinely close on Sundays. Alcohol can be purchased almost anywhere and anytime. Marijuana is increasingly becoming legalized for recreational use. LGBTQ people are now widely accepted in mainstream society, with the stigma once placed on this population quickly falling away. Even portrayals of Christians in entertainment have gone from generally positive to ignorant or outright negative. Setting aside whether each of these changes are contrary to the teachings of Jesus, or core to the Christian faith, this still represents a dramatic cultural shift in just a few decades.

Saying Christians are "under attack" also raises another question. Is the attack something to be feared? What is the specific danger? How can this attack hurt me? What do I stand to lose? Some Christians may answer this question with concerns about fewer people coming to know God. They fear more human suffering because cultural headwinds will keep people from having a relationship with God.

For many, there could also be another reason they fear the attack of culture. It is just uncomfortable. It is always more comfortable to spend time with your own tribe, people who believe as you do. This is why for much of history we have seen immigrant communities cluster together even in their new home nation. It is just easier, more comfortable, it feels like home. And for much of the past several generations, the United States has felt like home for Christians, especially white Christians. Besides being a faith, Christianity was also a proxy for a cultural sameness that just made things easier. Christians did not have to invest time in getting to know other religions, or even other cultures. Evangelism in the U.S. often meant leading someone who was taught Christianity as a child to come back to the faith as an adult. Christians did not need to learn how their beliefs contrasted with other religions, or even understand the foundation for their beliefs.

Even if the general U.S. population may not have been Christian in terms of having a living, vibrant relationship with God, it was at least Christian in terms of generally following the same rules and having the same customs. The U.S. was culturally Christian. That made it easy to call oneself a Christian. You could make the case that it also made Christianity weak. In the past couple of decades, the number of cultural Christians has declined, and more people choose not to follow any religion. And with that shift, the cultural bubble that made it so easy to be Christian has popped. It takes different muscles for faith to survive and thrive in a pluralistic society where not everyone sees the world the same way. And Christians in the U.S. have historically not had to build those muscles.

Ironically, today's Christians enjoy a level of religious liberty and social acceptance that would have been unthinkable in the time of Jesus. At the end of Jesus' earthly ministry, there were at most a few thousand Christians on the entire planet. Christianity was a new and unknown religion that fostered a radical view of God. In those times, almost all other religions in the Mediterranean and Middle East were polytheistic. These religions usually focused on a series of deities that each impacted life on earth in specific ways. A citizen in the Roman Empire might worship the god of war (Mars), the god of the weather (Jupiter), the goddess of fertility (Ceres), or any of the many gods in the Roman pantheon.[140] In addition, many cities had their own gods. And, as the Roman Empire expanded, it increasingly absorbed local gods and adopted or adapted them. A great deal of time and expense went into currying the favor of these gods. Peasants and emperors alike took great pains to try and please the gods, lest some misfortune come upon the non-compliant non-worshipers.[141]

In this world, Judaism stood as a dramatic outlier. In a far-flung corner of the empire called Judea, a people practiced a religion that worshiped what they called the one true God.[142] Only one God! Jewish people did not try to curry favor with the pantheon of gods, so they were easy targets when things went badly. "If those crazy Jewish people had only burned incense to Zeus, that storm would not have ruined our crops." Jews were a tiny minority, a few million people in an empire of tens of millions,[143] and were viewed with great distrust or even disdain.

And, within this small outcast minority of Jews was an even smaller group of just a few thousand people who followed a

Jewish teacher named Jesus, called Christ. It is almost impossible to overstate how tiny a minority the first Christians were, or how far outside the cultural and religious mainstream they lived.

Jesus embraced this underdog and outcast position.

> On one occasion, as Jesus was walking, someone said to him, "I will follow you wherever you go."
>
> But Jesus replied, "'Foxes have dens to live in, and birds have nests, but the Son of Man has no place even to lay his head.'"[144]

Jesus lived almost completely outside mainstream culture. He had no permanent home. Even the Jewish leaders, themselves a bit of a pariah minority within the broader empire, viewed Jesus as an outcast. He had no political power, no economic power. Yet, there is no evidence he viewed any of this as a liability in his pursuit of sharing the truth of God and impacting lives for the better.

> "'I have told you all this so that you may have peace in me. Here on earth you will have many trials and sorrows. But take heart, because I have overcome the world.'"[145]

Jesus demonstrated that the truth does not need to be in power to be powerful. Truth has the power to change hearts and minds no matter where the speaker fits in the social order.

So confident was Jesus in the power of truth, independent from the power of culture, that he sent his closest followers out into the community, then the broader world alone. He took this tiny minority of Christians and fragmented it even further by sending out small groups to other places.

> "Jesus called the Twelve together… and sent them out to proclaim God's kingdom and to heal the sick. They departed and went through the villages proclaiming the good news and healing people everywhere."[146]

Everywhere the followers of Jesus went, they were a tiny minority, still thriving, despite being outside the margins of the prevailing culture.

Jesus had very realistic expectations for how his followers would be received by society.

> He said, "'Look, I'm sending you as sheep among wolves. Therefore, be wise as snakes and innocent as doves. Watch out for people – because they will hand you over to councils and they will beat you in their synagogues. They will haul you in front of governors and even kings because of me so that you may give your testimony to them and to the Gentiles.'"[147]

Jesus did not see external attacks, the headwinds of culture, or even outright persecution, as things to be feared.

"'God blesses those who are persecuted for doing right, for the Kingdom of Heaven is theirs. God blesses you when people mock you and persecute you and lie about you and say all sorts of evil things against you because you are my followers. Be happy about it! Be very glad! For a great reward awaits you in heaven. And remember, the ancient prophets were persecuted in the same way.'"[148]

Earlier we mentioned that stating "Christianity is under attack" begged two questions, and now we apply those two questions to the person of Jesus Christ. First, we ask, "Who is attacking?" and for Jesus the answer was simple. Everyone. Everyone was attacking Jesus. Literally every aspect of society and culture was against him and his first followers. By comparison, any attacks on Christianity in today's United States is laughably minor by comparison. The second question is perhaps even more critical, "What do I have to fear from this attack?" Will this attack threaten my mission, my purpose in life? Will this attack derail God's plan?

In light of this attack, what should I fear?
For Jesus, the answer was resounding.
Fear no attack. Fear nothing at all.

17

"*Christians Think There Are Three Gods but Really One God?*"
The Trinity Relationship

Of all the theological aspects of Christianity, there may not be any more confusing than the concept of the Trinity. Christians believe that there is one God who exists in three persons: God the Father, God the Son, and God the Holy Spirit. One being with three manifestations. Jewish people view this as heresy and claim it suggests there is not just one God. Polytheistic religions point to this as evidence that Christianity is not really all that different. Atheists chalk this up to just one more bit of mystical nonsense. Even within the Christian faith, the interpretation of the definition of "Trinity" has driven countless debates, hurt feelings, even splits among congregations and denominations.

Although there is no record of Jesus ever using the term trinity, he did speak about these three manifestations of God on multiple occasions.

Jesus spoke about a Heavenly Father who knows us and cares

for us.

> "Then Jesus said to the crowds and to his disciples... 'Only God in heaven is your Father.'"[149]

> "'Look at the birds. They don't plant or harvest or store food in barns, for your heavenly Father feeds them. And aren't you far more valuable to him than they are?'"[150]

Jesus also spoke about a Holy Spirit of God that is with us every moment, guiding us, teaching us, and empowering us to live as Jesus did.

> "'The Companion, the Holy Spirit, whom the Father will send in my name, will teach you everything and will remind you of everything I told you.'"[151]

> "'...You will receive power when the Holy Spirit comes upon you. And you will be my witnesses, telling people about me everywhere...'"[152]

Finally, Jesus spoke about himself as the Son of God, whose mission it was to reconcile God and humankind.

> "'For this is how God loved the world: He gave his one and only Son, so that everyone who believes in him will not perish but have eternal life. God sent his Son into the world not to judge the world, but to save the world through him.'"[153]

Yet, although Jesus taught there were three aspects to God, he explicitly taught that there was only one God.

> "'The Father and I are one.'"[154]

> "Jesus replied, 'The most important commandment is this: "Listen, O Israel! The Lord our God is the one and only Lord."'"[155]

So how do we reconcile the concept of the trinity with the explicit teaching that there is only one God? This is probably one of those areas where the human mind finds itself at a loss to describe a divine reality. But a simplistic answer might be to think of the three persons of God as three roles or aspects of God. For instance, the same individual person can be a father to his children, a son to his parents, and a guiding spirit to those with whom he has shared wisdom or knowledge. The fact that the same person fills these three roles does not make him three different people. In this way, the Christian doctrine of a triune God existing in three persons does not conflict with the belief that there is only one God. Christianity, like Judaism, is monotheistic to the core.

Jesus taught about a single God who was all powerful and all knowing, who was bigger than anything we can see or imagine. But one of the most remarkable things about the concept of the trinity is how Jesus describes God in terms of relationship to mankind. Most other religions in the time of Jesus described God in relationship to nature. Many cultures would have a god of the sun, a god of the weather, a god of the sea, or a god of fertility. The primary focus of these gods was manipulating or controlling a natural process or pursuing their own objectives. Mankind at best was just an incidental victim of their choices. But Jesus described a God who was deeply concerned about and engaged with humankind.

> God the Father, who created everything, yet loves each person deeply and will go to great lengths to reconcile them to himself.

> God the Son, who walked the earth as a man, experienced all the pains and joys of being human, and chose to die on behalf of mankind.

> God the Holy Spirit, who is alive inside our hearts, giving us wisdom in every moment and showing us the way to God.

For those who have heard God described this way many times, the above may sound so familiar as to be mundane. But the contrast with the prevailing religions in the time of Jesus was dramatic. And the impact of this kind of teaching can be profound. A God, who is just some vague distant force, is something to be acknowledged, feared, and perhaps placated by my sacrifices and actions. That kind of God is not terribly relevant in my day-to-day life. But Jesus described a God that sought an active and intimate relationship with mankind.

> God the Father loves me and cares about me.

God the Son knows exactly what I am going through because he has lived as a human.

God the Spirit lives inside my heart to empower me in daily life.

The trinity is not just an esoteric religious framework – it is a roadmap for the relationship between one God and every individual human.

18

"Christians Think Jewish People Need To Be Converted"
The God Jesus Prayed To

"Whom do [the Jews] have to avenge the synagogue? Christ whom they have killed, whom they have denied? Or will God the Father avenge them, whom they do not acknowledge as Father since they do not acknowledge the Son?"

– Ambrose, bishop of Mediolanum, while trying to convince Roman Emperor Theodosius not to acknowledge the civil rights of Jews.[156]

"First to set fire to their synagogues or schools and to bury and cover with dirt whatever will not burn, so that no man will ever again see a stone or cinder of them. This is to be done in honor of our Lord

and of Christendom, so that God might see that we are Christians."
— Martin Luther, "The Jews and Their Lies" 1543.[157] [158]

The quotes above are likely as shocking to most modern Christians as they are disturbing to Jewish people. Anti-Jewish rhetoric and teaching has a long and shameful history in the Christian church. The past hundred years have seen a concerted effort by Christian leaders, Protestant and Catholic alike, to stamp out anti-Jewish and anti-Semitic teaching and attitudes among Christian churches. Yet the fruit of centuries of error remains. In 2008, a Pew research study found 42% of Jewish respondents felt hostility toward evangelical Christians.[159] [160]

Much of his hostility is likely rooted in historical efforts by Christians to convert Jewish people. In the first thousand years of Christianity, efforts to convert Jewish people were mostly grass roots, person to person efforts. Until around the twelfth century, the Catholic Church would accept Jewish converts, but did not widely engage in organized campaigns to convert Jewish people to the Christian faith. But, as the political power of the Christian church grew, attempts to convert the Jewish community became much more organized and widespread. These efforts often began peacefully but became more coercive over time. In medieval Europe, a Jewish person unwilling to convert might live as a second-class citizen in their own town, unable to do certain jobs or participate fully in society. In many cases, they would have their property destroyed, be beaten, or even killed.[161]

One of the most notorious examples is the widespread killing of Jewish people in the region now comprising Spain and Portugal in the fourteenth century. This led to a wave of Jewish people becoming baptized as Christians. A few decades later, the Catholic Church in Spain became skeptical as to whether these new converts were truly believers. As a result, they launched the Spanish Inquisition, which became one of the most bloody and shameful episodes in religious history.[162]

This history is widely known and understood by religiously devout Jewish people, as well as the culturally Jewish who are students of their own history. Over the centuries, the term "conversion" to many has become synonymous with oppression and even anti-Semitism. A Christian trying to convert a Jewish person to Christianity may feel like they are handing a friend a key to a new level of happiness and peace with God and man. But the Jewish person may feel they are being beaten with the same rod that oppressed their people for generations.

Reinhold Niebuhr said it bluntly:

> "Christian missionary activity among the Jews… are wrong not only because they are futile…. They are wrong because the two faiths despite differences are sufficiently alike for the Jew to find God more easily in terms of his own religious heritage than by subjecting him… to a faith… which must appear as a symbol of an oppressive majority culture… Practically nothing can purify the symbol of Christ as the image of God in the imagination of

the Jew from the taint with which ages of Christian oppression in the name of Christ tainted it."[163]

Acknowledging this history, and also reviewing the theological underpinnings of Christian views of Judaism, the Catholic Church issued statements in 1965 affirming the symbiosis between the faiths. In 2015, Pope Francis went as far as to prohibit any formal efforts to proselytize or convert people of the Jewish faith. Eugene J. Fisher, distinguished professor of theology at Saint Leo University and former head of the Secretariat for Catholic-Jewish Relations for the U.S. Conference of Catholic Bishops, has accurately summed up the current Roman Catholic position on attempts to convert Jews:

> "The Second Vatican Council declaration, Nostra Aetate... stresses that the covenant between God and the Jewish People, as the Bible states in many places, is 'irrevocable'. Both Jews and Christians are, equally, the People of God. The logical conclusion of this official Church teaching is that Jews do not need to convert to Christianity in order to be saved. They already are saved. Thus, the Church's approach to Jews cannot be to proselytize or try to convert them. It must be one of dialogue between two Peoples of God who are bound together by a common Bible, the Hebrew Scriptures, and the fact that Jesus lived and died a faithful Jew."[164]

Protestant Christian denominations vary in how they view Judaism. Some believe Jewish people must convert to Christianity in order to be saved, while others believe Judaism is a version of the same path to the same God. Perhaps the most famous and prolific Protestant Christian evangelist of the past century was Billy Graham. In 1973, he said:

> "I believe God has always had a special relationship with the Jewish people... In my evangelistic efforts, I have never felt called to single out Jews as Jews... Just as Judaism frowns on proselytizing that is coercive, or that seeks to commit men against their will, so do I."[165]

Of course, all of these Christian churches trace their origin to Jesus Christ. This compels us to contemplate where Jesus might have stood on the issue of converting Jewish people to Christianity.

Jesus was himself ethnically Jewish and a follower and teacher of Judaism. Jesus studied the Tanakh extensively, taught in the synagogue, observed Jewish days of remembrance and celebration.

> Jesus spent a great deal of time in the temple, even at an early age. "When Jesus was twelve years old... they... discovered him in the Temple, sitting among the religious teachers, listening to them and asking questions."[166]

Toward the end of Jesus' life, even after he had garnered so many followers, he still went to the synagogue regularly. In fact, at the time of his arrest, he said to those who came for him:

> "'Why didn't you arrest me in the Temple? I was there every day.'"[167]

Although Jesus had many rhetorical clashes with the Jewish religious leaders, and frequently challenged their methods and their motives, he affirmed the importance of their role in the overall structure of the Jewish faith.

> "'The teachers of religious law and the Pharisees are the official interpreters of the law of Moses. So, practice and obey whatever they tell you, [just] don't follow their example. For they don't practice what they teach.'"[168]

Jesus had a great affection for his own people. Near the end of his ministry, while walking on the outskirts of Jerusalem, he looked over the city and said:

> "'O Jerusalem, Jerusalem, the city that kills the prophets and stones God's messengers! How often I have wanted to gather your children together as a hen protects her chicks beneath her wings, but you wouldn't let me.'"[169]

Jesus also prioritized the nation of Israel in his ministry. Although he later charged his disciples with spreading the "good news" to "all nations," he initially sent them only to their own people, the Jewish people.

> "Jesus sent out the twelve apostles with these instructions: 'Don't go to the Gentiles or the Samaritans, but only to the people of Israel – God's lost sheep. Go and announce to them that the Kingdom of Heaven is near.'"[170]

Many Christians point to the following words of Jesus as proof that the Christian religion is a path to God and Judaism is not:

> "Jesus told him, 'I am the way, the truth, and the life. No one can come to the Father except through me.'"[171]

But this statement may not necessarily preclude Christians from viewing devout followers of Judaism as being in right standing with God. Christians and Jewish people alike believe that Judaism was ordained by God, and this religion was the primary way God revealed himself to mankind for thousands of years. Christians also believe that the key rituals and prophecies of ancient Judaism were an effective path to God precisely because they pointed toward the eventual arrival of a Messiah (Jesus) who would sacrifice himself to reconcile humanity to God. If that was true in the time of Moses, then it would still be true today. That would mean the canon and rituals of Judaism still point to the sacrificial life of Jesus. By that logic, Christianity and Judaism are parallel paths to God, each built on the same fundamental truth. And to use the words of Christians, in both paths, Jesus is still The Way.

Jesus made it very clear that he was not trying to replace Judaism.

He observed the Hebrew law, celebrated the occasions defined in the Torah. Jesus studied the Tanakh relentlessly, and much of his public speaking was based around passages from the Hebrew canon. He said:

> "'Don't even begin to think that I have come to do away with the Law and the Prophets. I haven't come to do away with them but to fulfill them.'"[172]

Jesus was building on top of the established truth revealed to the nation of Israel over thousands of years. He viewed his ministry as a fulfillment of the Hebrew Scriptures, not a replacement of them.

Note that Jesus did not instruct his disciples to tell their fellow Jewish people to renounce their faith or convert to a new religion. He told them to tell Israel that the "Kingdom of Heaven" was near. "Kingdom of Heaven" or "Kingdom of God" are terms used frequently by Jesus. This refers to embracing the reality of the power and authority of God on earth and living with a full consciousness of God's rightful place.[173]

> About a thousand years earlier, ancient Israel's greatest leader, King David, said this: "'Blessed are you, LORD, God of our ancestor Israel, forever and always. To you, LORD, belong greatness and power, honor, splendor, and majesty, because everything in heaven and on earth belongs to you. Yours, LORD, is the kingship, and you are honored as head of all.'"[174]

Jesus did not tell his disciples to spread the word of some new God to their nation, but to tell their own people that the God they already followed was drawing even closer to them.

So, what did Jesus command his followers to do as it relates to evangelizing others? In one of his last conversations with his disciples:

> "Jesus came near and spoke to them. 'I've received all authority in heaven and on earth. Therefore, go and make disciples of all nations, baptizing them in the name of the Father and of the Son and of the Holy Spirit, teaching them to obey everything that I've commanded you. Look, I myself will be with you every day until the end of this present age.'"[175]

The word 'baptizing' here is often interpreted to refer to the Christian ritual of someone having water sprinkled on them or being submerged in water as a testimony that they are a follower of God. And while this is an important ritual in the faith, and one affirmed by Jesus (he himself was baptized), this word actually has a much broader meaning. The original word that has been translated into English as 'baptize' means, "…to be immersed in, overcome with, or fully identified with."[176] Jesus was referring to something much bigger and more powerful than a water ritual.

Rather, Jesus was imploring his followers to help all peoples become fully immersed in the reality of all aspects of God. Jesus brought deeper revelation about the same God; he did not introduce a new God. And he wanted everyone, including the

Jewish people, to know God fully. Jesus said the key to doing this was to follow his teachings, so his disciples should teach people "to obey everything I have commanded you." In other words, Jesus commanded his disciples to do this: help people draw closer to God. This is perhaps the most succinct encapsulation of what Jesus saw as his core mission.

And the God he was referring to was the God of Abraham, the God his fellow Israelites had been worshiping for centuries, and still worship today.

19

"Christians Are Hypocrites"
Part 1: Relationship With Other People

"American Christianity... sent missionaries to other countries but refused to accept these same "foreigners" into their homeland... American Christianity promised eternal salvation in heaven while refusing to save refugees on earth... American Christianity claimed to be based on the pillars of truth and honesty, but endorsed politicians who lie and cheat. American Christianity pretended to worship the Prince of Peace while perpetuating endless wars across the world. American Christianity paid lip service to love and acceptance, but thrives on fear and oppression."[177]

– Stephen Mattoon

> *"In a survey of 3119 Americans aged over 18... half of those who described themselves as non-religious considered American Christians to be 'self-righteous,' 55 percent "hypocritical...' There was a 'fundamental disconnect' between the ways in which Christians saw themselves and how non-Christians viewed them, the... study found."*[178]
> — Ipsos Poll 2022

Perhaps the most common criticism of Christians is that they are hypocrites. Like the other criticisms we have discussed, this is certainly not true of all Christians. But it is true of enough of them that the public perception persists.

Of course, Christians have not cornered the market on hypocrisy. Hypocrisy is a disconnect between what you say you believe and what you do, a dichotomy between a standard and an action. And we find it across all faiths and cultures. People of all walks and faiths can be hypocritical, but for some reason the hypocrisy of Christians, the disconnect between actions and standard, seems even more offensive. Why is this?

The hypocrisy of Christians is different, not because their behavior is flawed – the action side of the equation. Everyone has flaws in behavior. The hypocrisy of Christians is different, seems even more unjust, because they claim to follow a standard that is higher and unique.

Christians claim their faith and their standards are exceptional, so we expect their behavior to be. Even those who do not believe in the deity of Jesus have great respect for how he lived his life. So, when there is a disparity between the standard set by Jesus and the actions of his followers, and the hypocrisy somehow seems even more offensive, even unjust.

Given how difficult it seems to be for Christians to live up to the words of Jesus, it is a fair question to ask how Christ himself lived up to his own words. We start by understanding the standard Jesus said we should live by. As we discussed earlier, his macro command only had two parts – love God and love your neighbor as yourself. When it comes to loving others, we see remarkable consistency between principles Jesus taught and the way he lived his life.

Jesus consistently showed love for everyone, especially those who the rest of society dismissed as flawed sinners. The Book of Mark provides a notable example:

> "Later, Levi invited Jesus and his disciples to his home as dinner guests, along with many tax collectors and other disreputable sinners. (There were many people of this kind among Jesus' followers.) But when the teachers of religious law who were Pharisees saw him eating with tax collectors and other sinners, they asked his disciples, 'Why does he eat with such scum?' When

> Jesus heard this, he told them, 'Healthy people don't need a doctor – sick people do. I have come to call not those who think they are righteous, but those who know they are sinners.'"[179]

Jesus did not reserve love and relationship for those who earned it with good deeds, but gave it freely to everyone.

Jesus even loved his enemies. The Pharisees were teachers and students of Hebrew law who continually harassed Jesus, tried to trick him into saying things that would alienate people, and eventually conspired to have him killed. Yet, one night one of these enemies came to have an open conversation with Jesus.

> "There was a man named Nicodemus, a Jewish religious leader who was a Pharisee. After dark one evening, he came to speak with Jesus. 'Rabbi,' he said, 'we all know that God has sent you to teach us. Your miraculous signs are evidence that God is with you.'"[180]

In the moments that followed, Jesus took the time to have a deep and meaningful discussion with this Pharisee. And it was in this conversation with an "enemy" that Jesus spoke perhaps the most famous words in the Bible.

> "Jesus replied… 'For this is how God loved the world: He gave his one and only Son, so that everyone who believes in him will not perish but have eternal life.'"[181]

Perhaps the most transparent example of Jesus loving others came in the final moments of his life when he had been beaten and hung on a cross.

> "When they came to a place called The Skull, they nailed him to the cross… Jesus said, 'Father, forgive them, for they don't know what they are doing.' And the soldiers gambled for his clothes by throwing dice."[182]

The people around Jesus had beaten him, mocked him, were trying to kill him, and were gambling over the clothes they had ripped from his body. Yet, he responded with love and forgiveness.

Jesus did not just love with words and sermons; he showed love by taking action. Jesus took care to understand the physical needs of people around him, and then took action to meet those needs.

> "Then Jesus called his disciples and told them, 'I feel sorry for these people. They have been here with me for three days, and they have nothing left to eat. I don't want to send them away hungry, or they will faint along the way.' …Then he took the seven loaves and the fish, thanked God for them, and broke them into pieces. He gave them to the disciples, who distributed the food to the crowd. They all ate as much as they wanted. Afterward, the disciples picked up seven large baskets of leftover food."[183]

Jesus also demonstrated love to others, even when that meant making his own needs secondary. On one occasion, someone close to Jesus (John the Baptist) was brutally murdered by the local Roman ruler. Jesus felt great grief and went away to be alone. But, when he saw people in need, he set his own needs and pain aside in order to meet the needs of others.

> "John was beheaded in the prison... As soon as Jesus heard the news, he left in a boat to a remote area to be alone. But the crowds heard where he was headed and followed on foot from many towns. Jesus saw the huge crowd as he stepped from the boat, and he had compassion on them and healed their sick."[184]

As it relates to his command to love others, it is impossible to find any hypocrisy in the accounts of the life of Jesus. He consistently put the needs of others ahead of his own needs and demonstrated love to everyone. The alignment of his words and deeds was absolute.

20

"*Christians Are Hypocrites*"
Part 2: Relationship With God

"Only 61% of Christians pray every day and 46% attend a religious service at least once a month."[185]

– *Pew Research Survey*

"Only 32% of Christians read the Bible every day."[186]

– *Lifeway Research Survey*

Earlier we saw the first of the two core commands of Jesus was to "...love the Lord your God with all your heart, with all your being, and with all your mind."[187] It is unrealistic and unfair to try and quantify the degree to which someone actually loves God. You cannot measure love. But, love does suggest a relationship. If I love someone, assuming they are alive and nearby, it follows that I would want to spend time with them, to talk to them, to hear what they have to say. These are core components of a relationship.

So, if I genuinely love God, it stands to reason I would spend time with him and be in conversation with him. Prayer and scripture reading are two key ways to do this, yet a substantial percentage of Christians do not regularly engage in these practices. This is a hypocrisy that is difficult to see but no less real, the hypocrisy of saying we love God when our actions and priorities suggest otherwise.

So, what about Jesus? Based on what we know about his actions, did he consistently follow the commandment to love God with all his heart?

Now the obvious first question might be, "Wait, but wasn't Jesus God? Doesn't this just mean he loved himself?" As we discussed earlier, the concept of the trinity is one of those areas that pushes the threshold of human understanding. But, while Jesus made it clear there is only one God, he also made it clear that within God are three aspects, three persons so unique as to have diverse ways of relating to humankind. Jesus claimed to be the manifestation of God in human flesh. But he was keenly aware of the conflict between the human nature common to his physical body and the divine person of God the Father. Jesus still had to choose to love God, the divine source from which his earthly existence had been born. And we see time after time, even though Jesus was subject to the temptations and weaknesses of humanity, his love for God the Father was absolute.

So, what does it really mean to love God? The idea of love between God and mankind is not something found in most religions. The starting point for many belief systems is transactional compliance, taking actions to garner favor from a god or set of cosmic principles that is, at best, indifferent to each individual. Fearing God, even obeying God, is relatively easy to understand. But love? Love between human and God is a profoundly difficult concept to grasp.

So how does a person demonstrate love for God, beyond simple compliance? Some faiths, even some Christian denominations, have complex rituals designed to demonstrate love for God. But, to understand the kind of love Jesus was referring to, a better reference point might be how we demonstrate love in a healthy relationship. How do you know when you love someone? There are many answers, but three things are usually prominent when you love someone.

- You want to talk to them, spend time with them.

- You want to know all about them.

- What is important to them becomes important to you.

Jesus consistently modeled all three of these in his relationship with God the Father.

First, Jesus spent a great deal of time talking to God. Or to use a religious term, Jesus prayed often. Luke records that, even as the fame of Jesus grew and there were even greater demands on his time, he still frequently took time away to talk to God.

> "...The report of his power spread even faster, and vast crowds came to hear him preach and to be healed of their diseases. But Jesus often withdrew to the wilderness for prayer."[188]

This often required a great deal of effort. Getting away from the crush of followers often required walking far into the wilderness or getting up very early.

> "Early in the morning, well before sunrise, Jesus rose and went to a deserted place where he could be alone in prayer."[189]

And these were not just short formulaic prayers, although a short prayer is infinitely better than no prayer. Jesus had extended conversations with God.

> "During that time, Jesus went out to the mountain to pray, and he prayed to God all night long."[190]

Another way to demonstrate love for someone is to put in the effort to get to know them. For Jesus, this took the form of reading the Tanakh to learn more about God. Jesus claimed to be God in human form, but he was not necessarily born with all the powers and knowledge of God. Luke says Jesus grew and developed like any other human.

> "The child grew and became strong and filled with wisdom – God's favor was upon him."[191]

This suggests that Jesus had to put in effort to unlock wisdom and knowledge of God. Jesus was born with gifts but had to put in work and time to unlock those gifts to the fullest. Jesus embraced that effort. By the time his ministry began, he had a command of scriptures that amazed even the most senior theologians of his day.

Another way we show love is by valuing what the people we love value. Jesus made it clear this was the core way we express love to God. In fact, when asked what people should say when they talk to God, Jesus mentioned this specifically.

> Jesus said, "'Pray like this: Our Father in heaven, may... your Kingdom come soon. May your will be done on earth, as it is in heaven.'"[192]

Jesus said his entire life purpose was aligned with doing what was important to God.

> "'For I have come down from heaven to do the will of God who sent me, not to do my own will.'"[193]

He further taught this alignment with the will of God was a hallmark of those who were children of God.

> "Looking around at those seated around him in a circle, [Jesus] said, 'Look, here are my mother and my brothers. Whoever does God's will is my brother, sister, and mother.'"[194]

But in contrast to so many other belief systems of the day, Jesus articulated a much different relationship between compliance and love. Obedience to the will of God was not a way to earn the love of God. God already loved humans. Obedience was a way to express love for God.

> "'If you love me, you will keep my commandments.'"[195]

Doing God's will is the outflow of a heart in love with God, valuing something that is valued by someone you love greatly.

Perhaps the ultimate testament to how much Jesus valued what God valued is found in the final days before his death. With his arrest and death imminent, Jesus asked God if there were any way to avoid that crucible. Yet, he ultimately embraced God's will, no matter the pain that meant for him personally.

> He said, "'Father, if it is your will, take this cup of suffering away from me. However, not my will but your will must be done.'"[196]

Whether you think Jesus was a delusional madman, God come to earth, or somewhere in between, you cannot deny his absolute devotion to doing the will of the God he loved.

Jesus spent time talking to God in prayer, learning about God in scripture, and following God's will even under impossible circumstances. He did all these things with a passion and commitment that is difficult to comprehend. He dedicated his life to these things because his love for God was absolute and unwavering. More than anyone who ever lived, Jesus embraced his first commandment to "love God with all your heart". We cannot find a shadow of hypocrisy in how Jesus related to God.

When the rest of the world complains about the hypocrisy of Christians, they are most often referring to hypocrisy in how Christians relate to other people. It is all too easy to name an occasion when a Christian fell short of Christ's command to "love your neighbor as yourself." By comparison, hypocrisy related to Christ's command to "love God with all your heart" is much less visible. It is difficult to know whether someone is really devoted to God. However, the teachings of Jesus suggest this mostly invisible hypocrisy is even more destructive.

When Jesus taught his two foundational commandments, he mentioned loving God first.

> "'…You must love the Lord your God with all your heart, all your soul, and all your mind. This is the first and greatest commandment. A second is equally important: Love your neighbor as yourself.'"[197]

This a clue to another core teaching of Jesus. Our love for other people is an outgrowth of our love for God. Jesus used the metaphor of a vine to make this point.

> "'Remain in me, and I will remain in you. A branch can't produce fruit by itself, but must remain in the vine. Likewise, you can't produce fruit unless you remain in me. I am the vine; you are the branches...'"[198]

In his relationships with others, Jesus was an incredibly generous, kind, and selfless person. But this love for others was not a cold act of will, driven from obligation. It was the natural overflow of the love that God had put in his heart.

> Jesus said, "'...A tree is identified by its fruit. Figs are never gathered from thornbushes, and grapes are not picked from bramble bushes. A good person produces good things from the treasury of a good heart, and an evil person produces evil things from the treasury of an evil heart. What you say flows from what is in your heart.'"[199]

The fruit of our lives is the impact we have on others, the imprint our words and actions have on the people around us. It is impossible to have a Godly impact without being connected to God. The innermost relationship with God is the source for the outermost interactions with other people. In this way, hypocrisy in the first commandment to love God is inextricably linked to hypocrisy in the second command to love others. The teaching of Jesus suggests that if Christians fail to fully love others, it is likely because they have first failed to fully love God.

Jesus anticipated a time when people who claimed to be pious followers of God would actually bring great pain to the earth. He cautioned against listening to those whose piety was grounded in rules and obligation rather than sourced from the love of God. On one occasion Jesus said,

> "'Watch out for false prophets. They come to you dressed like sheep, but inside they are vicious wolves. You will know them by their fruit. Do people get bunches of grapes from thorny weeds, or do they get figs from thistles? In the same way, every good tree produces good fruit, and every rotten tree produces bad fruit.'"[200]

Many people look at Christians and see rotten fruit – hypocrisy in how we relate to others. But what they cannot see is likely a greater hypocrisy – a lack of commitment to a relationship with God. Embedded in the simple core command of Jesus was the key to living a life free of hypocrisy. Love God first. Invest in a relationship with God first. A branch cannot yield fruit unless it is connected to the vine.

21

Mini-Christs and Major Truth

In these pages we have reviewed many things people dislike about Christians. And we found most of those things stand in sharp contrast to the example of Christ.

> Jesus did not impose a lot of rules.
> Jesus included everyone.
> Jesus sought out a diverse group of followers.
> Jesus almost never became angry.
> When Jesus was angry, it was usually at religious people.
> Jesus did not tell his followers to judge others.
> Jesus cared nothing about politics and culture wars.
> Jesus did not hate gay people.
> There is no record of Jesus talking about abortion.
> Jesus did not say Jewish people were going to hell.
> Jesus embraced science.
> Jesus was not fearful of being under attack.
> Jesus was not a hypocrite.

Unfortunately, many Christians are in many ways not like the Christ they follow. In the first century, when the followers of Jesus were first called Christians, it was meant as a term of derision. The original term can essentially be translated "Little Christs."

This term that was meant as a mockery is really the highest of callings. But Christians fall short of this calling in small and large ways every day. We can probably all agree with Nietzsche, who famously said,

> "There was only one Christian, and he died on the cross."[201]

In fact, a Buddhist or Muslim who is truly devout might often seem more Christ-like than a person who is just culturally Christian.

People who consider the person of Jesus in comparison to the behavior of Christians might have an instinct to condemn Christians as failures, untrue to their faith and unworthy of the name by which they call themselves. However, a core tenet of the teaching of Jesus is that being a failure does not mean being condemned. Likewise, true Christianity embraces even its most imperfect followers. Jesus taught that humans were flawed creatures, but that God loved them completely despite those flaws. He embraced imperfect people who acknowledged their imperfections.

Jesus said that an acknowledgment of our failure and our propensity to sin should be a core part of our prayer, our conversation with God.

He said, "'Pray like this: Our Father in heaven, may your name be kept holy... and forgive us our sins, as we have forgiven those who sin against us. And don't let us yield to temptation, but rescue us from the evil one.'"[202]

And Jesus promised that God would freely forgive our imperfections.

"'...Forgive, and you will be forgiven.'"[203]

Surely the grace that Jesus extended to everyone should be extended to his followers, no matter how imperfectly they follow.

So, rather than take the disconnect between Christians and Christ as an occasion to hate Christians, perhaps we should use it as an occasion to admire Christ. Even staunch atheists like author Fyodor Dostoyevsky find something to admire in Jesus. He said:

> "Even those who have renounced Christianity and attack it, in their inmost being still follow the Christian ideal, for hitherto neither their subtlety nor the ardor of their hearts has been able to create a higher ideal of man and of virtue than the ideal given by Christ of Nazareth."[204]

If a Christian reads these pages and feels something in their life or attitude should change, then I would encourage them to embrace that. Many of the words in these pages landed heavy on my own heart. We all come up short sometimes. We should all strive to more closely adhere to the ideals we value. But more than admonishing Christians, my greater hope is that this little book inspires people who are not Christians to take a closer look at the admirable person of Jesus Christ.

No matter how his name is used today, the selfless intent of Jesus was only to bring hope and good into the world.

> He said, "'The thief enters only to steal, kill, and destroy. I came so that they could have life – indeed, so that they could live life to the fullest.'"[205]

Jesus' reference to thieves is even more relevant today. There are so many thieves in our world. And the worst thieves are not the ones that want to take our money or possessions. Our society is overrun by thieves that want to steal our joy, our peace, our friendships, our hope, our mental health, our future. Some of these thieves are people, but many are ideologies, or attitudes, or organizations.

There are myriad voices who claim to know the truth, to speak for whatever god they are convinced is the highest form of life in the universe. It is one of the great contradictions of our time that so many disagree with each other, yet seem to have so much certainty that they alone are right and everyone else is wrong. Both secular and spiritual belief systems have become impossibly complex and militantly inflexible. People are willing to sacrifice principles for power, relationships for politics, charity for tribes, the sugar rush of being right for the much more difficult to obtain nourishment of showing love. The result is a society where everyone is absolutely right, which means everyone is also completely wrong. Virtuous love of our chosen tribe is tainted by hatred of the Evil Others. There is no room for humility of not knowing but wanting to know. There is no quarter for the simple acceptance of loving but not agreeing.

The irony is that, even in this environment of externalized disagreement and certainty, so many harbor the nagging doubt that maybe they do not have it all figured out. Even more feel an aching hope that there is a better way to live. But as the chaos and uncertainty in our world reaches a fever pitch, we are expected to hold the line that our chosen tribe is the one with the answers. To acknowledge the pain of the Evil Others means humanizing them to the point that they are worthy of compassion, and that does nothing to help my side win. But every time we double down on the "us versus them" narrative, every time we hide our doubts and pain under the bravado of tribe, we raise the walls between people a little bit higher. And that wall does not just isolate those who disagree with me, it isolates me as well.

In this environment, the simple truth Jesus taught stands in sharp relief and provides a beacon of hope. Jesus acknowledged the universal imperfection of humanity, the universal struggles and pain we face. But he did so by tearing down the barriers created by class, culture, tradition, economics, and even religion. Jesus taught and demonstrated loving embrace instead of judgmental rejection. In perhaps his most famous sermon, Jesus said the following:

> "'God blesses those who are poor and realize their need for him, for the Kingdom of Heaven is theirs.
> God blesses those who mourn, for they will be comforted.
> God blesses those who are humble, for they will inherit the whole earth.
> God blesses those who hunger and thirst for justice, for they will be satisfied.
> God blesses those who are merciful, for they will be shown mercy.
> God blesses those whose hearts are pure, for they will see God.
> God blesses those who work for peace, for they will be called the children of God.
> God blesses those who are persecuted for doing right, for the Kingdom of Heaven is theirs.'"[206]

Jesus did not describe people who were the finished product, who had everything all figured out. Most of the characteristics he mentions above are transient states.

> Blessed are those who recognize they need God, that there are things they do not know.
> Blessed are those that mourn, because it will not always be so.
> Blessed are those who seek justice, because justice will come.
> Blessed are those who work for peace because that is when we are most like God.
> Blessed are those who suffer for doing the right thing.

That sermon acknowledges an imperfect world, a humanity that is a work in progress. But it is full of so much hope. Those truths are incredibly relevant today, and exactly what our world needs to hear.

To go a little further, consider the two core commands of Jesus we addressed earlier. "Love God with all your heart." Dare to believe there is something bigger, something above all the noise, something worthy of complete devotion. "Love your neighbor as yourself." Fully embrace who you are and love others extravagantly. Actively seek to help others.

Those are commands that can change the world. Jesus spoke truths that can change hearts for the better. What a shame it would be for people to never hear those truths over the din of culture warfare. What a tragedy it would be if the people who take Jesus' name become an obstacle to hearing his words.

Jesus has a lot to say that all of us need to hear.

My hope for these pages is that, even if some of us have been alienated or hurt by Christians, we can look beyond the failures of Christians to find hope in the Unchristian Christ.

Endnotes

[1] Proverbs 27:17 (New Living Translation) NLT
[2] https://www.pewforum.org/2021/12/14/about-three-in-ten-u-s-adults-are-now-religiously-unaffiliated/
[3] John 3:16-17 (Common English Bible) CEB
[4] https://www.quora.com/Is-Christianity-real-or-is-it-just-another-way-to-control-the-masses
[5] https://www.simplycatholic.com/introduction-to-canon-law/
[6] Liberty Way Student Honor Code, p. 11. https://www.liberty.edu/students/wp-content/uploads/sites/89/2022/10/The-Liberty-Way.pdf
[7] https://www.pewresearch.org/fact-tank/2019/03/06/americans-drinking-habits-vary-by-faith/
[8] https://www.frc.org/booklet/the-ten-commandments-foundation-of-american-society-
[9] https://www.pewresearch.org/religion/2010/09/28/us-religious-knowledge-an-overview-of-the-pew-forum-survey-results-and-implications/
[10] https://www.chabad.org/library/article_cdo/aid/756399/jewish/The-613-Commandments-Mitzvot.htm
[11] Mark 2:27 (*CEB*)
[12] Matthew 22:35-40 (*CEB*)
[13] https://www.quora.com/Why-do-some-religious-people-evangelise-rather-than-just-leaving-everyone-to-believe-whatever-they-want
[14] https://www.spurgeon.org/resource-library/sermons/good-cheer-for-outcasts/

[15] https://www.usatoday.com/story/news/nation/2021/02/28/white-nationalists-use-christian-symbols-send-messages-racists/4457702001/

[16] https://bible.org/illustration/hatred-between-jews-and-samaritans

[17] John 4:24 (*CEB*)

[18] Racially Diverse Congregations in the U.S. Have Nearly Tripled in the Past 20 Years, Baylor University Study Finds https://www.baylor.edu/mediacommunications/news.php?action=story&story=220972

[19] Multiracial Congregations Have Nearly Doubled, But They Still Lag Behind the Makeup of Neighborhoods https://www.baylor.edu/mediacommunications/news.php?action=story&story=199850

[20] https://research.lifeway.com/2019/09/26/heading-into-2020-elections-most-evangelicals-want-to-play-nice-in-politics/

[21] Acts of the Apostles 4: 13 (*CEB*)

[22] Mark 8: 33 (*NLT*)

[23] John 18:15-18 (*NLT*)

[24] Mark 3:16-17 (*NLT*)

[25] Luke 8 1-3 (*CEB*)

[26] https://www.patheos.com/blogs/keithgiles/2020/08/the-forgotten-female-disciples-of-jesus/

[27] John 10:14, 16 (*CEB*)

[28] https://medium.com/@wterrya/why-are-christians-so-angry-98f6b95f818f

[29] https://www.quora.com/Why-do-so-many-Christians-seem-so-angry?top_ans=353951228

[30] Ephesians 4:26-27 (*CEB*)

[31] Mark 3:1-5 (*CEB*)

[32] https://www.bibleodyssey.org/passages/main-articles/jesus-and-the-money-changers-john-213-16/

[33] https://www.learnreligions.com/jesus-clears-the-temple-bible-story-700066

[34] John 2:13 - 17 (*CEB*)

[35] Matthew 21:13 (*CEB*)

36 Matthew 23:13, 23-25, 27-28 (*CEB*)

37 Matthew 5:38 - 39 (*CEB*)

38 Luke 9:53-56 (*CEB*)

39 Luke 10:25-37

40 Luke 23:14-15, 18, 21-24, 33 *CEB*

41 Luke 23:34 (*CEB*)

42 Matthew 5:43 - 44 (*CEB*)

43 https://frenchpress.thedispatch.com/p/christian-political-ethics-are-upside?triedSigningIn=true

44 Luke 4:5 - 8 (*CEB*)

45 John 6:15 (CEB)

46 Matthew 15:18 - 19 (Contemporary *English Version*)

47 Matthew 22:37 - 40 (*CEV*)

48 Matthew 22: 16 - 17, 19 - 22 (*NLT*)

49 https://quotefancy.com/quote/870784/Napoleon-I-know-men-and-I-tell-you-that-Jesus-Christ-is-not-a-man-Superficial-minds-see-a

50 Justin Lee, Torn: Rescuing the Gospel from the Gays-vs.-Christians Debate

51 https://journals.sagepub.com/doi/abs/10.1177/0146107915577097?journalCode=btba

52 https://www.livingout.org/resources/articles/18/what-does-the-bible-say-about-homosexuality

53 https://zondervanacademic.com/blog/have-we-misunderstood-romans-1-on-gay-sex-6-evaluations

54 https://www.hrc.org/resources/what-does-the-bible-say-about-homosexuality

55 Leviticus 18:21 - 24 (*CEB*)

56 http://religiousinstitute.org/denom_statements/homosexuality-not-a-sin-not-a-sickness-part-ii-what-the-bible-does-and-does-not-say/

57 Romans 1:26 - 27 (*CEB*)

58 Matthew 19:4 - 6 (*CEB*)

[59] Matthew 19:10 - 12 (*Complete Jewish Bible*)
[60] Matthew 22:23 - 30, 33 (*CEB*)
[61] Matthew 22:33 (*CEB*)
[62] https://www.pewresearch.org/fact-tank/2018/01/22/american-religious-groups-vary-widely-in-their-views-of-abortion/
[63] Aristotle, Politics 7.16 https://www.bbc.co.uk/ethics/abortion/legal/history_1.shtml
[64] Matthew 10:29 - 31 (*CEB*)
[65] Matthew 19:13 - 14 (*CEB*)
[66] https://pubmed.ncbi.nlm.nih.gov/12340403/
[67] Psalms 139:13, 16 (*CEB*)
[68] Jeremiah 1:5 (*CJB*)
[69] Genesis 2:7 (*CEB*)
[70] Exodus 21:22 - 23 (*CJB*)
[71] Numbers 5:12, 15, 18-22, 27 (*CEB*)
[72] https://www.quora.com/Why-are-Christians-considered-the-most-judgmental-religious-group
[73] The Barna Research Group and The Fermi Project, "A New Generation Expresses its Skepticism and Frustration with Christianity." September 2007. https://www.barna.com/research/a-new-generation-expresses-its-skepticism-and-frustration-with-christianity/
[74] Matthew 7:1 (*CEB*)
[75] Luke 18:9 - 14 (*CEB*)
[76] https://www.washingtonpost.com/news/acts-of-faith/wp/2017/08/03/christians-are-more-than-twice-as-likely-to-blame-a-persons-poverty-on-lack-of-effort/
[77] https://www.reddit.com/r/exchristian/comments/e7v7a0/i_am_so_fucking_sick_of_the_christian_victim/
[78] John 9:2 - 3 (*CEB*)

79 Matthew 25:34 - 46 (*NLT*)

80 Luke 24:47 (*NLT*)

81 John 8:3 - 11 (*CEB*)

82 John 3:17 (*CEB*)

83 Matthew 9:13 (*CEB*)

84 https://www.reddit.com/r/DebateAChristian/comments/5cmsdk/why_do_christians_wish_to_impose_their_views_on/

85 Luke 11:46 (*CEB*)

86 Luke 5:3-6, 8 -11 (*CEB*)

87 John 10:14 (*CEB*)

88 https://www.quora.com/Why-do-some-religious-people-evangelise-rather-than-just-leaving-everyone-to-believe-whatever-they-want

89 https://allthatsinteresting.com/who-wrote-the-bible

90 https://www.jewishvirtuallibrary.org/the-tanakh

91 https://textandcanon.org/why-the-catholic-bible-has-more-books-than-the-protestant-bible/ - :~:text=The Roman Catholic Bible has,the Protestant Bible contains 66

92 https://www.learnreligions.com/when-was-the-bible-assembled-363293

93 https://textandcanon.org/why-the-catholic-bible-has-more-books-than-the-protestant-bible/#:~:text=The%20Differences,-Catholics%20and%20Protestants&text=Thus%2C%20Catholics%20have%20seven%20more,additions%20to%20Daniel%20and%20Esther

94 https://csbible.com/read-the-csb/verse-comparison/

95 Matthew 5:17 (*CEB*) / (*CJB*)

96 O'Neal, Sam. "When Was the Bible Assembled?" Learn Religions, Aug. 31, 2021. https://www.learnreligions.com/when-was-the-bible-assembled-363293

97 John 12:49-50 (*CEB*)

98 Matthew 7:24 (*CEB*)

99 Matthew 24:35 (CEB)

100 Matthew 28:19-20 (*Amplified Bible*)

[101] https://digitalcommons.liberty.edu/cgi/viewcontent.cgi?article=1060&context=second_person
[102] Matthew 19:5 - 8 (*NLT*)
[103] Matthew 5:38 - 39, 43 - 45 (*NLT*)
[104] Luke 2:41 - 47 (*CEB*)
[105] Matthew 4:2 - 6 (*NLT*)
[106] John 3:16 (*CEB*)
[107] John 1:1 - 5 (*CJB*)
[108] https://www.gotquestions.org/Jesus-Word-God.html
[109] Luke 23:32 - 33, 39 - 43 (*CEB*)
[110] Acts 2:1 - 31 (*CEB*)
[111] https://kyleorton.co.uk/2021/06/11/how-many-christians-were-there-in-the-roman-empire/
[112] Rodney Stark, 1996, The Rise of Christianity, pp. 7 - 10.
[113] Mark 12:24 (*NLT*)
[114] John 8:32 (*NLT*)
[115] Matthew 7:28 - 29 (*NLT*)
[116] https://www.quora.com/profile/Bruce-Doran-1
[117] https://www.lexico.com/en/definition/scientific_method?s=t
[118] Mark 9:23 (*NLT*)
[119] John 11:40 (*NLT*)
[120] Matthew 13:58 (*NLT*)
[121] Luke 7:18 - 19, 22 (*NLT*)
[122] Luke 5:12 - 14 (*NLT*)
[123] https://bibliescienceguy.wordpress.com/2018/04/25/what-does-jesus-think-of-science/
[124] Luke 8:4 - 8, 10 (*CEB*)
[125] https://www.britannica.com/biography/Johannes-Kepler
[126] Romans 1:20 (*CEB*)
[127] Matthew 13:14 - 16 (*CEB*)

[128] Luke 11:52 (*CEB*)

[129] John 13:7 (*CEB*)

[130] Proverbs 25:2 - 3 (*NLT*)

[131] https://www.sagu.edu/thoughthub/faith-vs-science-can-these-two-co-exist/

[132] https://www.famousscientists.org/great-scientists-christians/

[133] https://www.goodreads.com/quotes/tag/open-mindedness

[134] Romans 1:20 (*NLT*)

[135] https://www.nbcnews.com/id/wbna12079836

[136] https://www.prri.org/research/fractured-nation-widening-partisan-polarization-and-key-issues-in-2020-presidential-elections/

[137] https://www.quora.com/How-exactly-are-Christians-under-attack-in-the-Unitedhttps://www.quora.com/How-exactly-are-Christians-under-attack-in-the-United-States-States

[138] https://www.theguardian.com/commentisfree/2022/mar/18/are-white-christians-under-attack-in-america-no-but-the-myth-is-winning

[139] https://news.vanderbilt.edu/2022/11/22/religious-liberty-has-a-long-and-messy-history/

[140] https://www.worldhistory.org/Roman_Religion/

[141] https://www.worldhistory.org/article/851/the-extent-of-the-roman-empire/

[142] https://www.thattheworldmayknow.com/religious-movements-of-jesus-time

[143] https://www.haaretz.com/2005-04-29/ty-article/study-traces-worldwide-jewish-population-from-exodus-to-modern-age/0000017f-e7d1-d97e-a37f-f7f53ba50000

[144] Luke 9:57 - 58 (*NLT*)

[145] John 16:33 (*NLT*)

[146] Luke 9:1 - 2, 6 (*CEB*)

[147] Matthew 10:16 - 18 (*CEB*)

[148] Matthew 5:10 - 12 (*NLT*)

149 Matthew 23:1,9 (*NLT*)

150 Matthew 6:26 (*NLT*)

151 John 14:26 (*CEB*)

152 Acts of the Apostles 1:8 (*NLT*)

153 John 3:16-17 (*NLT*)

154 John 10:30 (*NLT*)

155 Mark 12:29 (*NLT*)

156 https://www.ushmm.org/research/about-the-mandel-center/initiatives/ethics-religion-holocaust/articles-and-resources/christian-persecution-of-jews-over-the-centuries/christian-persecution-of-jews-over-the-centuries

157 https://www.iwu.edu/history/constructingthepastvol9/Paras.pdf

158 https://christianhistoryinstitute.org/magazine/article/was-luther-anti-semitic

159 https://www.city-journal.org/html/why-don%E2%80%99t-jews-christians-who-them-13068.html

160 https://www.jewishboston.com/read/do-you-think-its-possible-for-someone-to-be-both-jewish-and-christian-in-some-real-sense/

161 https://www.jstor.org/stable/2864373

162 https://www.newyorker.com/news/news-desk/pope-francis-and-the-renunciation-of-jewish-conversion

163 The Relation of Christians and Jews In Western Civilization, CCAR Journal (April 1958), 18-32.

164 https://religionnews.com/2019/09/27/christian-churches-own-up-to-the-futility-of-converting-the-jews/

165 https://religionnews.com/2019/09/27/christian-churches-own-up-to-the-futility-of-converting-the-jews/

166 Luke 2:42, 46 (*NLT*)

167 Luke 22:53 (*NLT*)

168 Matthew 23:2-3 (*NLT*)

169 Matthew 23:37 (*NLT*)

170 Matthew 10:5 - 7 (*NLT*)

171 John 14:6 (*NLT*)

172 Matthew 5:17 (*CEB*)

173 https://www.str.org/w/what-is-the-kingdom-of-heaven-

174 1 Chronicles 29:10 - 11 (*CEB*)

175 Matthew 28:18 - 20 (*CEB*)

176 https://redeeminggod.com/no-water-baptism-in-matthew-28_19-20/

177 https://christiansforsocialaction.org/resource/american-christianity-hypocrisy-problem/

178 https://www.churchtimes.co.uk/articles/2022/18-march/news/world/american-christians-seen-as-hypocritical-and-judgemental-study-suggests

179 Mark 2:15 - 17 (*NLT*)

180 John 3:1 - 3 (*NLT*)

181 John 3:1 - 3, 16 (*NLT*)

182 Luke 23:33 - 34 (*NLT*)

183 Matthew 15:32, 36 - 37 (*NLT*)

184 Matthew 14:10, 13 - 14 (*NLT*)

185 https://www.pewforum.org/2021/12/14/about-three-in-ten-u-s-adults-are-now-religiously-unaffiliated/

186 https://research.lifeway.com/2019/07/02/few-protestant-churchgoers-read-the-bible-daily/

68% of white evangelicals believed that the United States "does not have a responsibility" to house refugees...The highest level of support from any group cited in the study was from those who identified as religiously unaffiliated, of whom a full 65 percent support American housing of refugees.

187 Matthew 22:37 (*CEB*)

188 Luke 5:15 - 16 (*NLT*)

189 Mark 1:35 (*CEB*)

190 Luke 6:12 (*CEB*)

191 Luke 2:40 (*CJB*)

[192] Matthew 6:9 - 10 (*NLT*)

[193] John 6:38 (*NLT*)

[194] Mark 3:34 - 35 (*CEB*)

[195] John 14:15 (*CEB*)

[196] Luke 22:42 (*CEB*)

[197] Matthew 22:37 - 39 (*NLT*)

[198] John 15:4 - 5 (*CEB*)

[199] Luke 6:43-45 (*NLT*)

[200] Matthew 7:15-17 (*CEB*)

[201] https://www.goodreads.com/quotes/6014-in-truth-there-was-only-one-christian-and-he-died-on

[202] Matthew 6:9, 12 - 13 (*NLT*)

[203] Luke 6:37 (*CEB*)

[204] *Fyodor Dostoevsky (2017). "The Brothers Karamazov (English Russian Edition illustrated): Братья Карамазовы (англо-русская редакция иллюстрированная)", p.402, Clap Publishing, LLC.*

[205] John 10:10 (CEB)

[206] Matthew 5:3 - 10 (*NLT*)

Made in the USA
Middletown, DE
26 April 2023

29304212R00109

FROM 2014 TO 2021, the percentage of adults in the U.S. who identified themselves as Christians declined from 78% to 63%. This means about 49 million fewer people associated themselves with the religion built on the teachings of Christ.

And while it is difficult to find anyone who has something negative to say about the life and teachings of Jesus of Nazareth, a quick internet search for "What do you dislike about Christians?" returns a litany of complaints and objections.

What if we reviewed the most common complaints about Christians, and compared those to what we know about Jesus of Nazareth? Would Jesus himself feel at home in the ranks of today's Christians? Or would he be too Unchristian for the religion that calls him Christ?

KERRY MORRIS is not a theologian or pastor, but he has been an intentional and imperfect follower of Jesus for over forty years. He is a businessperson and a writer whose work leads him to thousands of interactions annually, mostly with people who do not profess to be Christian. This project was driven by a deep desire to understand different perspectives, and passion for the kind of truth that shines brighter under the light of scrutiny. Kerry lives in the Atlanta, Georgia, area with his amazing wife, three wonderful children and one habitually problematic dog.